Two Texas Race Riots

Fred L. McGhee, Ph.D.

Fidelitas Publishing
Austin, Texas

Published by Fidelitas Publishing
2316 Thrasher Lane
Austin, TX 78741-6622

Cover: The M1903 Springfield Rifle played a prominent role in the investigation of the Brownsville Raid. Image by *Curiosandrelics* and furnished under the GNU Free Documentation License.

Library of Congress Control Number: 2012950182

ISBN 978-0-615-62879-0

Printed in the United States of America

Contents

Preface

The goal of this monograph is to furnish a brief summary of two important racially charged and nationally significant events in black history, military history, and Texas history. By their very nature, both events remain controversial and are usually not taught in Texas schools, public or private. It is the author's hope that this easy-to-read publication can help to rectify that situation.

The scholarly literature about the Black experience in Texas authored by African Americans themselves remains disquietingly underdeveloped. The book also fills an important gap in the Afro Texas history literature by furnishing a modern African American interpretation of these events.

The narrative can also be appreciated as a mostly matter-of-fact description of two inherently dramatic American race conflicts that took place during the early Jim Crow era. The Shakespearean nature of both the 1906 Brownsville Riot and the 1917 Houston Riot require little in the way of dramatic embellishment.

The book is broken into two parts. The first part concerns itself with the 1906 Brownsville Raid and contains a brief summary statement followed by a more developed but still succinct narrative description of events. Part two, which follows the same format, is about the 1917 Houston Riot.

For more information, including teacher curriculum assistance and continuing education credit opportunities with the author, visit http://www.twotexasraceriots.com.

Acknowledgements

For helpful comments and assistance, I thank John Griggs, Jodi Skipper, Turkiya Lowe, Susan Ferentinos, and Carol McDavid.

For illustrations and general support I thank the University of Texas at Brownsville and Fort Sam Houston National Cemetery.

For inspiration and love I thank Lisa Goddard, Theresia McGhee, Carmen Ratzel, and Carmen McGhee.

A Brief Word about the Racial Climate of Early Twentieth Century America

Historians have referred to the early Jim Crow era in American history (1890-1920) as the "nadir" of American race relations.[1] It was an era that reduced black Americans to second class citizenship and whose virulent racial bigotry seems almost extraordinary by contemporary standards. Segregation increased everywhere. Lynchings and racial terror were daily facts of life for the majority of African Americans. Mass media representations of blacks depicted them as clowns, monkeys, buffoons or children, and these depictions applied to all blacks, regardless of educational achievement or professional status. When Jack Johnson, a Texan who counted several members of the Buffalo Soldiers as friends, became the first African American to win the world heavyweight title in 1908, the resulting racist media barrage against him was so severe it launched the "great white hope" era in boxing.[2] Jim Jeffries, the greatest of the white hopes, left his alfalfa farm and lost 100 pounds to come out of retirement to face Johnson. On July 4, 1910 Johnson knocked Jeffries out in the fifteenth round on a hot day in Reno, Nevada. Blacks across the country celebrated the victory; whites responded with violence. In the riots that followed all across America, as many as 26 people were killed and hundreds injured, the majority of them black.

Racially motivated incidents of this nature were an unfortunate fact of American life in the early twentieth century. The nationwide riots that followed the Jack Johnson and Jim Jeffries heavyweight fight were preceded by the Atlanta Race Riot and the Brownsville, Texas incident in 1906 as well as racial incidents in Onancock, Virginia in 1907 and Springfield, Illinois in 1908. The Houston Riot of 1917 was preceded by the 1917 East St. Louis Riot, which contributed to the already simmering racial tensions responsible for the conflagration in Houston.

Race riots reached their peak with the Red Summer of 1919, during which several U.S. cities, including Chicago, Washington, D.C., Charleston and others experienced significant property damage and loss of life. In most of these incidents white mobs attacked African-American neighborhoods and citizens.

Perhaps the most elucidative incidents of racial violence from this period are the 1921 Tulsa Race Riot and the 1923 Rosewood Massacre in Florida. The Tulsa race riot was a large-scale racially motivated conflict between the white and black communities of Tulsa, Oklahoma, beginning May 31, 1921. During the 16 hours of the assault, over 800 people were admitted to local hospitals with injuries, an estimated 10,000 were left homeless, and 35 city blocks composed of 1,256 residences were destroyed by fire caused by bombing. The Greenwood neighborhood of Tulsa, known as "Black Wall Street," was wiped out. The Rosewood Massacre took place in early January 1923 when several hundred white Floridians destroyed the mostly quiet and black town of Rosewood, Florida.

The Brownsville Riot of 1906 and the Houston Riot of 1917 must be seen, therefore, within a context of racial violence, much of it extreme and most of it committed by white Americans against black citizens. We thankfully currently live in era where the legal machinery of segregation has been largely disassembled, but in visiting this era of American history I ask the reader to make a special effort to appreciate events in historical as well as contemporary terms, but also to make an effort to answer the question demanded by a serious engagement with history: What would I have done?

CHAPTER ONE

A Brief History of the Buffalo Soldiers Infantry Up to World War One

The origins of what would later be known as the "Buffalo Soldiers" lie in the Civil War, when various regiments of United States Colored Troops were organized for the Union war effort. Black soldiers served with distinction, and after the war the Wilson Act of 1866 established six regular army black regiments, the first such peacetime regiments in U.S. history. The regiments consisted of the 9th and 10th cavalries and the 38th, 39th, 40th and 41st infantries. Two of the infantry units were eliminated and combined into the 24th and 25th infantries (colored) in 1869.

To the disappointment of black soldiers and their advocates, the army assigned white officers to command the regiments, limiting black upward mobility. Service discrimination in the army and racism in society at large held that blacks did not possess the character and leadership skills necessary to lead troops, black or white. Additionally, in the early years of the regiments' existence, most white officers regarded service leading black troops as highly undesirable; for example George Custer famously refused to lead black troops.[1]

The etymology of the term "Buffalo Soldier" is not entirely clear. The consensus opinion appears to be that Plains Indians such as the Cheyenne and Comanche used the designation as a sign of respect for the soldiers, and for their hair texture, which the Indians thought resembled the hair of the buffalo.[2]

Buffalo soldier infantry service along the western frontier was highly challenging. Black soldiers found themselves stationed in such desolate locations because these assignments were considered some of the least attractive posts in the military. Largely relegated to guarding remote outposts in the Indian west, the servicemen also found themselves performing an array of other tasks beyond garrison duty, such as digging ditches and fortifications, stringing telegraph lines, guarding survey teams and stagecoaches, and other aspects of fort maintenance, all within a context of stifling racial prejudice and hatred from both army personnel as well as many of the locals.[3]

In their early years, the Buffalo Soldier infantry regiments acquired little of the glory attached to the two cavalry regiments, which distinguished themselves in important Indian skirmishes, and one of which was briefly led by the first black graduate of West Point, 2nd Lieutenant Henry Ossian Flipper. Between bursts of excitement, the infantrymen basically experienced endless hours of tedium, marked by incessant drills, inspections, rigid discipline, and maintenance of forts erected in an unforgiving environment.[4]

The black troops acquitted themselves well. Unlike white troops stationed in remote outposts who frequently succumbed to alcoholism or who deserted, the black soldiers handled the boredom and "hurry up and wait" conditions of frontier service with aplomb. Genuinely proud in their status as American soldiers, most of the servicemen had few opportunities— economic or otherwise—as civilians in post Civil War America and their service on the Western frontier was borne of duty, not race hatred of Indians. During the last three decades of the nineteenth century the Twenty-fourth infantry had the lowest desertion rate of any unit in the U.S. Army, despite being outfitted with cast-off military equipment and the tendency of the Army to mete out harsher punishments to black soldiers for minor transgressions.

The outbreak of the Spanish-American War gave the regiments their first sustained opportunity to demonstrate their mettle in battle. The War Department, under the assumption that blacks "possessed a natural immunity to tropical heat and diseases" mustered all four regiments in Florida in 1898 to await immediate shipment to Cuba. During their stay in Tampa, the members of the Twenty-fourth and Twenty-fifth endured the customary and unfortunate litany of racial insults from the local press, citizens, as well as from fellow soldiers. Racial tensions were so bad the men were not allowed to go ashore to bathe or exercise unless an officer accompanied the entire company.[5] They also intervened when a group of Ohio volunteers "decided to have some fun" with a two year old black boy by using the frightened youngster for target practice. The Ohio soldiers repeatedly shot at the boy, but did not kill him, while his hysterical mother looked on helplessly. The Buffalo Soldiers intervened. The so-called "Tampa Riot" of June 6, 1898 resulted in the wounding of at least twenty-seven soldiers and three white volunteers.[6]

All four Buffalo Soldier regiments served in Cuba with distinction. They charged up San Juan Hill with Theodore Roosevelt and helped propel him to national prominence. The Twenty-fourth regiment was given the honor of occupying Fort San Juan after the surrender of the Spanish forces.[7] Overall, however, the Buffalo Soldier regiments were disappointed when the recognition they thought due them was once again denied them. Roosevelt later found it politically expedient to deny that his "Rough Rider" volunteer regiment had been saved by the Tenth Cavalry, and to the consternation of black soldiers and civilians alike, he summarily dismissed an entire battalion of black infantrymen from the Army following the incident at Brownsville in 1906.[8]

Between 1899 and 1915 the Twenty-fourth completed three tours of duty in the Philippines. It was a difficult tour of duty for some of the soldiers, who felt conflicted about participating in an imperial war in which the Filipinos were called "Niggers" by white troops and their commanders. "In contrast to the low desertion rates of [blacks in] the Indian wars and the Mexican border conflicts, African Americans who served in the Philippines Islands deserted more than the whites, with some deserters even joining the insurrectionists against the U.S. Army."[9] In spite of these challenges, most of the members of the regiment served in an exemplary fashion and earned the respect of their officers, although the soldiers were removed early and out of rotation from the islands by the first civil administrator of the new colony William Howard Taft, because of the close rapport between the two colored races (Filipinos and blacks).[10]

After completion of their third Philippines tour, elements of the Twenty-fourth then rejoined the Ninth and Tenth in Columbus, New Mexico, as part of a punitive force under General John J. Pershing, a legendary Army officer whose command of the Tenth Cavalry earned him the nickname "Nigger Jack" (later softened to "Black Jack") during his tour as an instructor at West Point in 1897. Members of the regiment saw relatively little action during the 1916-1917 "Punitive Expedition" into revolutionary Mexico to intercept and harass Pancho Villa and his forces. President Wilson ordered the withdrawal of American troops from the area in early 1917.

President Wilson requested, and Congress granted, a declaration of war against Germany in April of 1917. In a sign of disrespect to the long tenured and distinguished Buffalo Soldier regiments, U.S. officials refused to send the troops to Europe to participate in the fighting. The military either sent colored troops of the regular army to non-war zones overseas or assigned them to menial duties within the United States. In a further insult, the War Department insisted on stationing the regiments in the Jim Crow south, against the wishes of the soldiers and their officers and usually over the objections of elected officials and business leaders in the cities themselves. "The Twenty-fifth Infantry spent the early months of the war in Hawai'i, and the Ninth Cavalry was ordered to the Philippine Islands, but the Twenty-fourth was broken up into three separate battalions and ordered to perform guard duty at three new camps designed to accommodate the training of national guardsmen being called into active service."[11] The Twenty-fourth's Third Battalion, consisting of Companies I, K, L, and M left Columbus, New Mexico on July 26, 1917 for Houston to guard the construction of Camp Logan, a newly funded National Guard training facility located about one mile west of the city's western outskirts.

CHAPTER TWO

A Brief Summary of the 1906 Brownsville Riot

On November 5, 1906, 167 African American enlisted soldiers of companies B, C and D of the 25th United States Infantry Regiment, Colored, were discharged "without honor" by order of President Theodore Roosevelt following a midnight raid in Brownsville, Texas that left one dead and two wounded.[1] Though the number of raiders was considered to be less than 20, all of the soldiers were deemed guilty, either through direct involvement or as participants in a "conspiracy of silence" to shield the aggressors. Unlike the two white officers charged in relation to the incident who were not disciplined, none of the enlisted men were afforded the presumption of innocence or provided with an opportunity to present a defense in a court-martial.[2] The discharged soldiers, who by all accounts had exemplary records of military service prior to the riot—many were distinguished veterans of the Spanish-American War—were barred from re-enlisting in the Army, Navy or the federal government and denied retirement benefits.[3] When they were finally vindicated in 1972, only two were still alive.[4]

CHAPTER THREE

The 1906 Brownsville Riot

Background

Organized in 1869, the Twenty-fifth Infantry comprised black enlisted personnel and usually white commissioned officers. Many of its early members were former slaves and Civil War veterans. Throughout most of the final decades of the 19th century, the Twenty-fifth was deployed on the western frontier. During the 1880's its members formed part of the Army's Bicycle Corps, which famously trekked from Montana to Missouri in 1897 in an experiment to test the military utility of bicycles. The following year, the regiment served with distinction in the Spanish American War, charging Kettle Hill alongside then Colonel Theodore Roosevelt and his Rough Riders during the Battle of San Juan Hill in Cuba. Shortly thereafter the regiment fought in the Philippines Insurrection.[1] It returned to the mainland United States in 1902 and was stationed at Fort Niobrara, Nebraska. In 1906 companies B, C and D of the Twenty-fifth Infantry were ordered to Fort Brown, Texas, the oldest post on the Rio Grande.[2]

Established in 1846, Fort Brown was situated along the Rio Grande at the southernmost tip of Texas, just across the border from the Mexican town of Matamoros. Originally comprising only earthworks, the fort was converted into a 358.8-acre military reservation after the Civil War. The adjacent town of Brownsville, founded in 1848, had a population of approximately 6,000 when the Twenty-fifth arrived on July 28, 1906.[3]

The Town of Brownsville

Fort Brown and the town of Brownsville were founded during the "Manifest Destiny" period of American history, and its establishment was conducted within a context of profound racial tension between "Anglo-Saxon" Americans and "Mongrel" Mexicans. The fort, known in its early days as "the camp near Matamoros," played a key role in the Mexican-American War and was the location of the Mexican Siege of Fort Texas, which took place between 3-9 May, 1846 and was the first active campaign in that war.[4]

The city of Brownsville was established in 1848 by Charles Stillman, a New Yorker who organized a partnership to purchase approximately fifteen hundred acres of a Spanish land grant for a town site on the north bank of the Rio Grande. At the time, the Mexican town of Matamoros across the Rio Grande was the senior and more populous settlement in the region. The period between the Mexican-American War and the Civil War saw a land and slavery boom in Texas, with Brownsville one of the principal beneficiaries. Even though Matamoros continued to surpass the younger community in size and economic importance, immigration of adventuresome and entrepreneurially minded Europeans and Americans led to a steady increase in the town's population and gave the town a strange admixture of frontier "western" feeling alongside the more refined air of a more cosmopolitan port city.[5]

The Civil War produced an economic and demographic upturn in Brownsville, as Texas cotton was smuggled across the border to circumvent the Union blockade. The town's population swelled to over twenty-five thousand settlers, who developed sophisticated smuggling and blockade running networks that entailed the transshipment of large quantities of cotton to the newly organized frontier boomtown of Bagdad in the Mexican state of Tamaulipas across the Rio Grande. The population explosion did not include enslaved African Americans; prior to and during the Civil War slaveowners hesitated to bring their property to Texas border towns for fear that they might scurry across the border.[6] British and French ships laid in anchor offshore and were supplied by river boats.[7] Given Brownsville's importance as a lifeline of the Confederacy in the latter Civil War years, the racial climate of the town during Reconstruction and the remainder of the nineteenth century was a decidedly Southern one. Racial attitudes towards blacks amongst the majority Hispanic population ranged from quiet acceptance or ambivalence to outright Southern style racial hostility, particularly on the part of Tejano elites, many of whom had been longtime landowners in the area. By and large, the town's Mexican population sought acceptance from the white leadership by assuming orthodox Southern views while also enhancing their limited social mobility at the expense of the town's few black residents.[8]

Following the Civil War Brownsville entered a period of relative decline, as cities such as Galveston and Houston grew. Never a significant cotton port outside of the Civil War, the local economy in the 1880's and 90's largely consisted of banditry and the occasional Chisholm Trail cattle drive. Hurricanes, yellow fever epidemics and cross-border intrigue—with the Porfirio Díaz regime for instance—were other major features of the time period. City boosters viewed railroad expansion as the path to the future and pushed hard for what would eventually become the St. Louis, Brownsville, and Mexico Railroad. That railroad was chartered in June 1903, and its first segment, a line between Brownsville and Robstown, Texas, was completed about 13 months later. The completion of the railroad produced the desired effect; by the time the soldiers of the Twenty-Fifth Infantry arrived in Brownsville in 1906, the city had re-embarked on a path of economic and demographic growth. Because of the sizable Hispanic element, the social and economic system relied on a more complex version of white supremacy than in the old south, but its features and mores were unmistakably recognizable as Jim Crow segregationist. Racial and class subjugation were the basis of social, political and economic life.[9]

The Lead-Up

The rigid and severe racial climate of Texas was a microcosm of the national racial atmosphere. At the turn of the century no average week went by without at least one or two lynchings.[10] When President Theodore Roosevelt, later to play a prominent role in the Brownsville Affair, dined with the African American leader Booker T. Washington in the White House on October 16, 1901, he was vilified and the meeting set off a firestorm of racial reaction. Newspaper headlines roared "Roosevelt Dines a Darkey" and "Our Coon-Flavored President." South Carolina Senator Ben Tillman said "The action of President Roosevelt in entertaining that nigger will necessitate our killing a thousand niggers in the South before they will learn their place again."[11]

Buffalo Soldier regiments were not strangers to frontier Texas of the post-Civil War era and were thus not unfamiliar with Texas racial hostility, particularly on the Mexican border. Three incidents, one in Laredo, one in Rio Grande City, and the other in El Paso preceded the affray in Brownsville. Members of the Twenty-Fifth Infantry were involved in two of the incidents, with the Ninth Cavalry involved in the other. Each encounter followed allegations from soldiers of racial discrimination and police harassment, countered by citizens' complaints of obnoxious military conduct. The Laredo incident took place in October, 1899 and involved members of Company D of the Twenty-Fifth Infantry, who assaulted a peace officer; the conflict in Rio Grande City took place in November 1899 and involved members of Troop D of the Ninth Cavalry who fired on the town; the last incident took place in February 1900, when enlisted men of Company A, Twenty-Fifth Infantry killed a lawman in El Paso. In each case—and unlike the Buffalo Soldiers stationed in Texas during the Indian Wars—the soldiers were recent and unwelcome arrivals who had proved their distinguished fighting spirit in Cuba and elsewhere. Unfortunately the soldiers' hard-won respect and "New Negro" twentieth century race pride came into conflict with the tightening grip of Jim Crow in Texas and elsewhere, creating conditions for a racial powderkeg.[12]

Though certain members of the white Twenty-Sixth Infantry regiment that was stationed at Fort Brown before the Twenty-fifth had advertised that the incoming black soldiers were "pretty good sort of fellows," their words fell on deaf ears. As before, pervasive racism and xenophobia among the primarily white and Mexican residents of Brownsville led to problems almost immediately.[13] Within days of the arrival of the black battalion from Fort Bliss (a stopover point from Nebraska), one soldier was pistol whipped for allegedly refusing to yield the sidewalk to white ladies, while another was abused by federal customs collectors. Adding insult to injury, local bars either closed their doors to the soldiers or forced them to drink in back rooms. Yet the men of the Twenty-fifth remained calm and refused to retaliate.[14] In fact, Brownsville police officers testified that their conduct was better than that of the white soldiers of the Twenty-Sixth Infantry who preceded them.[15]

A more serious problem arose on Sunday, August 12, two weeks after the soldiers had arrived. One of the town's red-light district white women, Mrs. Lon Evans, claimed that a "large Negro" wearing an Army uniform had seized her by the hair and thrown her violently to the ground before fleeing into the night. Word of the alleged attack spread quickly through the town, spurred by a provocative headline in the local newspaper: "INFAMOUS OUTRAGE: Negro Soldier Invaded Private Premises Last Might and Attempted to Seize a White Lady."[16]

At the request of the husband of the woman who was allegedly assaulted, the town's mayor, Dr. Frederick Combe, went to Fort Brown and met with the commander of the battalion, Major Charles Penrose. Penrose indicated that he did not believe that any of his men were capable of such an act, but assured the mayor that he would investigate. Before leaving, the mayor asked Major Penrose to confine his men to the post for the night. Penrose agreed and also agreed to impose an eight o'clock curfew on his men.[17]

The Raid

The raid began shortly before midnight on August 13, 1906. Allegedly, shots were fired into the air from Fort Brown, and then a number of men, variously estimated from five to twenty, climbed over the walls of the fort and began randomly firing into houses. While roaming the streets, the soldiers were confronted by a mounted police officer. Bullets killed his horse and smashed his arm, eventually requiring amputation. During the raid, the men also fired at other police officers and towards a group headed for a saloon that refused to permit them to drink alongside whites. The barkeep attempted to close the door to the saloon but was fatally shot.[18]

Major Penrose, Fort Brown's commanding officer, was awake in his quarters at the time. He heard two shots, by almost all accounts pistol fire, followed by a volley six or seven more from high-powered rifles. The shots seemed to him to have come from the north side of the Company B barracks (Figure 3.1). He believed the fort was under attack from the residents of Brownsville. The shooting continued as Major Penrose ordered that the men retrieve their rifles and assemble for roll call. All of the soldiers were accounted for except one of the white commissioned officers who slept through the affray. Within about ten minutes the raid was over, although Penrose kept the troops deployed in a defensive position for about an hour afterwards until a detachment of soldiers confirmed that the fort was not actually under attack. None of the officers saw among the men any signs of excitement or hard breathing, which would have suggested that they had rushed back to the reservation fresh from a riot a few blocks away.[19] Approximately 200 to 300 shots had been fired.[20] Though Major Penrose had no reason to suspect his men had participated in the raid—indeed he never considered that his men had engaged in an attack on the town until the mayor called on him later that night—he took the precaution of ordering that all rifles be locked up until daybreak when there would be sufficient light to inspect them. The inspection revealed no evidence that the weapons had been fired. All ammunition was accounted for as well.[21]

Private Joseph Howard, the sentinel guarding the area closest to the wall, later testified under oath that the gunfire came from outside the fort. Believing the fort to be under attack, he fired three shots into the air to sound the alarm. Matias Tamayo, the post scavenger, was emptying ash cans when he heard the gunfire, and similarly swore that the shooting took place outside the wall and assumed an attack on the garrison.[22]

Nonetheless, the following morning police discovered in the streets cartridges and ammunition clips for the Springfield '03 rifles recently issued to the Twenty-Fifth Infantry.

The raid resulted in the death of Frank Natus, a bartender at the Ruby Saloon who was shot by "a group of five or six men" who entered through a back door facing Cowan's Alley. One bullet fired by the raiders at the saloon also grazed the arm of Paulino Preciado, the editor of a local Spanish-language newspaper. Also wounded during the raid was police lieutenant M.Y. "Joe" Dominguez. He was shot in the arm as he rode away from the disturbance on horseback.[23]

The residents of Brownsville were convinced from the outset that the raid was perpetrated by enlisted soldiers of the Twenty-fifth. Though Brownsville was pitch dark on the new moon night of August 13, several individuals claimed to have seen the black raiders wearing uniforms and carrying Army-issue Springfield rifles. In addition, residents and one of the white officers had found shells and clips for Springfield rifles scattered on the ground along the route followed by the raiders. This led Major Penrose to believe that some of his men were guilty, though later, after a careful consideration of all the facts of the case, he proclaimed their innocence.[24]

By noon of August 14, the residents of Brownsville had formed a fifteen-member citizens' committee to investigate the raid. The investigation was a farce; the witness statements were not sworn and testimony was coached.[25]   By August 18, the Army had sent its own investigator, Major A. P. Blocksom, the Division Inspector General.   Blocksom spent eleven days in Brownsville and concluded, based on the statements made to the Citizens' Committee, that "the raiders were soldiers of the Twenty-fifth Infantry," despite the fact that no one could identify a single individual as responsible.[26]   The troops, claimed Blocksom, under a "conspiracy of silence" declined to name any of their fellows as guilty, even when advised that a refusal to do so would result in the collective punishment of the battalion, resulting in their discharge without honor, barring them from reenlistment in the Army, Navy, or civil service and denying them pension or benefits.

Despite glaring contradictions and inconsistencies in the testimony provided by the residents of Brownsville, the following case against the soldiers was cobbled together by Blocksom and others. Shortly before midnight on August 13, 1906, from five or six to twenty soldiers somehow managed to retrieve their Springfield rifles from secured gun racks, and implemented a premeditated plan to shoot up the town of Brownsville. They began by opening fire on the town from the porch of B barracks, then jumped the brick wall north of the barracks and proceeded up Cowan alley, firing into houses, hotels and saloons, including the Ruby Saloon where Frank Natus was killed and Paulino Preciado was wounded. Reaching Thirteenth Street, the raiders wounded police lieutenant M. Y. "Joe" Dominguez and fatally shot his horse. The raiders then headed west on Thirteenth Street to Washington Street. Turning south on to Washington Street, the raiders returned to the fort, shooting along the way.[27]

Blocksom's rush to judgment was based on the extremely questionable testimony of Brownsville citizens who claimed to have personally witnessed the rioting soldiers, including a nearly blind man who claimed to have seen the soldiers 150 feet away on a pitch black, moonless and starless night.[28]   Given the prevailing racial climate in Texas and the country at large, virtually

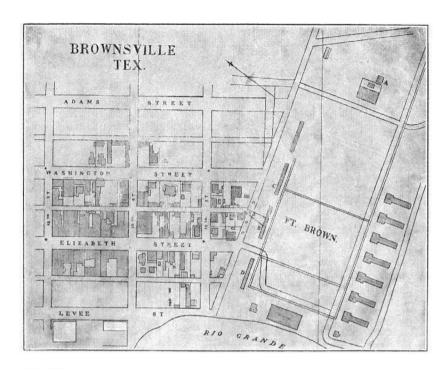

FIGURE 3.1. Map showing the northern portion of Fort Brown and downtown Brownsville.[25]   The enlisted men of the Twenty-fifth Infantry occupied the barracks labeled B, C and D, according to company. The white commissioned officers lived in the T-shaped buildings at lower right. Cowan's Alley, the focus of the raid, is between Elizabeth and Washington streets. Courtesy UT Brownsville Archives.

overnight every interested party beyond Brownsville accepted the city's and Blocksom's version of the facts as an open and shut case. The *Houston Post, Dallas Morning News,* and *Austin Statesman* ran almost identical front-page stories on August 15 in tones representative of southern journalistic norms.   "A dastardly outrage was committed against the people of Brownsville," stories began, "...by a squad of about twenty negro soldiers...who came from Fort Brown armed with Krag-Jorgenson rifles for the purpose of raiding the town."[29]   The next day on August 16, the editors of the *Austin Statesman* opined that the soldiers, if permitted to stay "should be treated as common curs and not men and when not under the eye of their masters they should be rendered harmless by the taking away of all arms and other

FIGURE 3.2. Photo of one of the barracks occupied by the enlisted men of the Twenty-fifth Infantry.[27] Army investigators alleged that certain enlisted men began the riot by shooting into the town of Brownsville from the porch of B barracks. The men then allegedly jumped the brick wall (visible to the right) which separated the military reservation from the town, and proceeded up Cowan's Alley.

instruments that would permit of them doing physical harm to their superiors."[30]

From the 15th to the 20th of August, 1906 the *San Antonio Daily Express* published various appeals from the citizens of Brownsville pleading for the removal of the black troops, which further poisoned the atmosphere and made a fair and impartial investigation of the affray almost impossible. "Our women and children are terrorized," claimed these Brownsvillians, "and our men in constant alarm and fearfulness; please remove Negro troops and replace them with white troops; send state troops; do something right away, for we are scared to death."[31]

On August 21, three days after Major Blocksom began his investigation, a storied Texas Ranger named Bill McDonald arrived in Brownsville by train from Dallas. Almost a caricatured embodiment of the "Texas law man," McDonald was infuriated that the investigations were taking so long and that none of the soldiers was sitting in jail. Though he had been denied permission by the Adjutant General to investigate federal soldiers, McDonald could not resist the opportunity to "go down and settle that Brownsville business"[32]   and proceeded to conduct his own rather haughty investigation.   An unabashed racist of the old school, McDonald soon came to the conclusion that the raid had been conducted by enlisted men of the Twenty-fifth Infantry. He secured bench warrants from a local judge for twelve of the men and one black ex-soldier, Ernest Allison, who, with financial backing from Private John Holloman of B Company, had opened a saloon in Brownsville that catered to the men of the Twenty-fifth. When the military refused to turn over the soldiers to McDonald's custody, he angrily told the judge "Judge, those niggers are not going to be moved from here.   They are my prisoners, and I'm going to hold them."

Shortly before the warrants were issued, Major Penrose received orders to relocate the Twenty-fifth to Fort Reno, Oklahoma.   On the day the battalion was preparing to leave, McDonald arrived at Fort Brown to demand custody of the men named in the warrants.   Sensing a lynching, Penrose refused to comply.   Instead, he informed McDonald that the men would be locked up in the post guardhouse.   Once McDonald left, Penrose cabled his commanding general to request permission to move the prisoners to safer confines in San Antonio.   The general granted the request, and shortly thereafter the presiding judge forced the Texas Ranger to return the bench warrants. Infuriated, McDonald left Brownsville empty-handed.[33]

The soldiers who had been arrested were incarcerated in San Antonio for over a month.   During this time a grand jury was convened in Cameron County to determine if there was adequate evidence to indict them.   While the members of the grand jury were convinced that the raid was perpetrated by soldiers of the Twenty-fifth, they were forced to conclude that "the evidence did not point with sufficient certainty to any individual or individuals to justify or warrant them in bringing in an indictment..."   As a result, the men were released and rejoined the battalion in Fort Reno.[34]

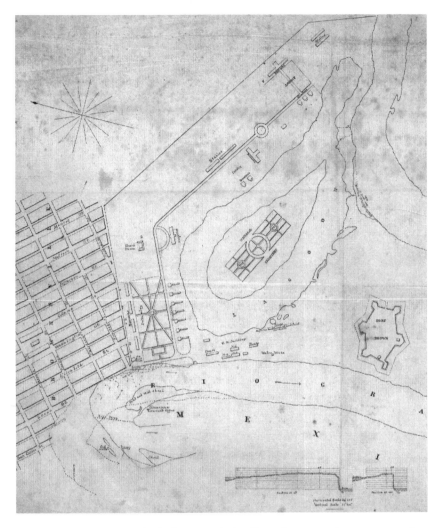

FIGURE 3.3. Detail of 1869 map of the Fort Brown military reservation showing principal buildings and original earthworks (lower right). Courtesy UT Brownsville Archives.

Despite the absence of evidence linking soldiers of the Twenty-fifth to the Brownsville affray, the Army was determined to pursue the matter. Two additional investigations followed. The first, conducted by Lieutenant Colonel Leonard A. Lovering, failed "[to] develop any material facts germane to the main issue," and proved of little consequence. The second was led by General Brigadier Ernest Garlington. This investigation, the first to have access to sworn statements from the soldiers, was equally unfruitful, but unlike Lovering's, it resulted in serious consequences. Based in large part on Major Blocksom's initial report, Garlington determined that the soldiers were guilty beyond reasonable doubt – though by his own admission he did "not procure any evidence thereof" – and recommended that all enlisted men in the battalion "should be found guilty of the shooting and of the concealment of the facts connected therewith, and be discharged without honor."[35] Paradoxically, he concluded his report by contradicting his own finding of culpability: "In making this recommendation I recognize the fact that a number of men who have no direct knowledge as to the identity of the men of the Twenty-fifth Infantry who actually fired the shots on the night of the 13th of August, 1906, will incur this extreme penalty."[36]

President Theodore Roosevelt eagerly accepted General Garlington's recommendations but was concerned about the implications of discharging the soldiers on the eve of elections for key seats in the House of Representatives. Republicans, including Roosevelt, had traditionally enjoyed the support of African Americans and were acutely aware of the possibility that news of the discharge could translate to defeats at the polls. Consequently, Roosevelt signed the order but delayed its release until November 7, 1906, long enough for the Republicans retain control of the House.[37] By the time of the election Roosevelt was on the presidential yacht for a trip to Panama to inspect America's new canal. Designated Special Order, No. 206, the President's judgment was as follows:

By direction of the President, the following-named enlisted men who, on August 13, 1906, were members of Companies B, C, and D, Twenty-fifth Infantry, certain members of which organizations participated in the riotous disturbance which occurred in Brownsville, Tex., on the night of August 13, 1906, will be discharged without honor from the Army of their respective commanding officers and forever debarred from reenlisting in the Army or Navy of the United States, as well as from employment in any civil capacity under the Government.[38]

The following day, the *New York Age* reported on the incident:

> The action is one of the most drastic ever taken by the President and is sure to cause a sensation throughout the service....this action of President Roosevelt is sure to arouse the bitterest surprise and anger everywhere among Afro-Americans. They believe that the Afro-American soldiers were heroic in refusing to betray their comrades to an unfair trial and certain death, and that they are merely another sacrifice offered by the President upon the altar of Southern race prejudice.[39]

Somewhat ironically, even Senator Ben Tillman of South Carolina called it an "executive lynching."[40]

One of the soldiers discharged was First Sergeant Mingo Sanders, a twenty-six year veteran of the Indian Wars and the Philippines who had also served with distinction with Roosevelt in Cuba. He was within a couple of years of retirement at three-quarters pay when he was sent packing by the man, now President, with whom he had shared some hard tack on June 25, 1898.[41]

The summary discharge, unprecedented in U.S. military history, sent political shockwaves across the nation.[42] Condemnation rained down on the president from both black and white journalists, black churches, and black political organizations such as the newly formed Niagara Movement.[43] W.E.B. Du Bois attacked Roosevelt for "swaggering roughshod over the helpless black regiment whose bravery made him famous," and even Booker T. Washington, long in Roosevelt's back pocket (and secretly notified of the impending order on October 30), attempted to intervene by asking Roosevelt to set aside the summary discharge of the entire block of soldiers, later declaring "I did my utmost to prevent his taking the action he did."[44] Black religious leaders such as Reverend Adam Clayton Powell, Sr. of Harlem's Abyssinian Baptist Church urged their members to seek vengeance at the polls in the next presidential campaign: "Once enshrined in our hearts as Moses" sermonized Powell, Roosevelt was "now enshrined in our scorn as Judas."[45]

In their 1908 denunciation of the Republican party, Du Bois, Frederick L. McGhee and other members of the Niagara movement urged black voters thusly:

Remember that the conduct of the Republican party toward Negroes has been a disgraceful failure to keep just promises. The dominant Roosevelt faction has sinned in this respect beyond forgiveness. We therefore trust that every black voter will uphold men like Joseph Benson Foraker, and will leave no stone unturned to defeat William H. Taft. Remember Brownsville, and establish next November the principle of Negro independence in voting, not only for punishing enemies, but for rebuking false friends.[46]

Reaction from fellow Buffalo Soldiers stationed elsewhere was similarly negative. In December, 1906 Vance H. Marchbanks, a squadron Sergeant Major with the 10th Cavalry wrote a letter from his post at Fort Washkie in Wyoming about his impressions of the incident. His dispatch, titled "A Soldier's Opinion of the Recent Excitement at Brownsville, Tex." is a unique document and furnishes useful insight into the state of mind of educated and experienced Negro opinion about the incident. Having himself been stationed at Ft. Brown in 1899, Marchbanks wrote that he was "well acquainted with the sentiment of its people" and observed that "the majority of the inhabitants of that section are a class that think a colored man is not good enough to wear the uniform of a United States soldier—yea not good enough even to wear the skin of a dog." After relating a story about his unfortunate run-in with a menacing Texas Ranger while on a recreational trip to Point Isabel (Marchbanks was on the Pt. Isabel train with a white woman), Marchbanks furnishes his opinion about the place of Negro soldiers in Brownsville:

A colored man who has the disposition of a toad frog (I mean one who can stand to be beaten on the back and puff up and take it), is all right; he can stay in that country. But those who feel hot blood running through their veins, and who are proudly and creditably wearing the uniform of a United States soldier; standing ready to protect and defend the American flag against any enemy whomsoever, to obey the orders of the president of the United States and the orders of the officer appointed over them (which they have always done with pride and honor), cannot stay down there in peace with honor.

At the same time, most white observers exulted in the humiliation of the black troops, and viewed the incident as confirmation of their racial theories. Some southern newspapers editorialized support for Roosevelt, despite having excoriated him only a few years earlier for dining with Booker T. Washington at the White House.[47] "Whatever may be the value of Negro troops in time of war," the New Orleans Picayune commented in a typical southern editorial, "the fact remains they are a curse to the country in time of peace."[48]

The Constitution League of the United States, an interracial civil rights organization, conducted an independent investigation and on December 10, 1906 submitted a report to congress that accused all of the investigating agencies of having presumed the guilt of the soldiers and of having failed to give them a fair hearing. The report was instrumental in persuading Senator Joseph B. Foraker, an Ohio Republican and presidential candidate, to champion the cause of the soldiers, although his critics insisted he was motivated more by ambitions for the Presidency than by a desire to correct an injustice.[49]

Following a thorough review of the facts of the case, Foraker concluded that the enlisted men of the Twenty-fifth Infantry could not have been responsible for the Brownsville raid. In late 1906 he introduced a resolution directing the Secretary of War,

William Howard Taft, to furnish all of the Brownsville records for investigation.[50]

The Senate investigation was conducted by the Military Affairs Committee, of which Foraker was a member, and took place between February 4, 1907 and March 10, 1908. Over the course of the investigation, Foraker deconstructed the case against the soldiers, capitalizing on testimony presented in the courts-martial of two white commanders of the Twenty-fifth, Major Penrose and Captain Macklin, who were charged and court martialed—and subsequently acquitted—of negligence in connection with the riot.[51] Apart from demonstrating that the testimony of the Brownsville residents was not credible, Foraker employed forensic analysis to prove that rifle shells found on the streets of Brownsville could not have been fired on rifles. Further, he provided evidence suggesting that townspeople or outsiders had staged the raid to banish the black troops or to avenge customs enforcement.[52]

On March 11, 1908, the committee issued three reports, a majority report and two minority reports. The majority report, authored by five Democrats and four Republicans, concurred with Roosevelt's determination that the men were guilty, either as perpetrators of the riot or participants in a conspiracy of silence to protect the perpetrators. As historian John Weaver observed, this conclusion was clearly based on politics rather than fact:

> In effect, the five southern Democrats found them guilty of being black, the four Republicans of having embarrassed the President and the man most likely to succeed him by refusing to confess to a crime no loyal party member cared to think they might not have committed.[53]

Each of the minority reports was authored by two Republicans. One concluded that the soldiers were "not guilty." The other, penned by Foraker, declared that "the weight of the testimony shows that none of the soldiers of the Twenty-fifth U.S. Infantry participated in the shooting affray."[54]

Despite the outcome of the investigation by the Military Affairs Committee, Foraker resolved to keep the Brownsville issue alive and possibly force some concession for the soldiers from President Roosevelt. Ironically, the ammunition he needed was provided by a member of Roosevelt's own administration, Wiliam Howard Taft. As Secretary of War, Taft had been involved in the investigation of the riot from the beginning. He recognized the weakness of the government's case against the soldiers and was desperate to find evidence that would put the matter to rest in the run-up to his campaign to succeed Roosevelt as president. Consequently, when Taft was approached in April of 1908 by a newspaper editor who offered to reveal who was behind the riot, he immediately contracted the man, Herbert J. Browne, and his assistant, William G. Baldwin, a private investigator. Unfortunately for Taft, however, the two men were con artists. Over the next several months, Browne and Baldwin bilked government funds while concocting false testimony against certain soldiers of the Twenty-fifth which they attributed to Boyd Conyers, one of the enlisted men in the regiment.[55]

After learning of the confession, Senator Foraker began his own investigation and determined that Conyers had been framed. In January of 1909, he presented a scathing attack on the Brown-Baldwin report in the Senate chamber.[56] On March 3, 1909, Roosevelt's and Foraker's last day in office, the president approved a court of inquiry composed of five retired Army generals that would decide whether any of the discharged soldiers qualified for reenlistment.[57] Under the rules set up by the War Department a soldier who desired reinstatement could apply to the court and submit evidence of his innocence, almost an impossible task and a reversal of presumption of innocence rights.

Though the court of inquiry offered some hope for justice, Senator Foraker realized that the possibilities were limited, not only because the officers involved were sympathetic to the Army's case, but also because the soldiers would be required to demonstrate that they were not guilty, a difficult proposition by any measure. On April 6, 1910, the generals, all white, revealed their findings. All five agreed that men under the command of Major Penrose were involved in the riot, and four were of the opinion that the incident could have been prevented if the officers and men of the battalion would have performed their respective duties immediately prior to the riot. Yet for reasons that were not divulged, the officers of the court also determined that fourteen of the enlisted men were qualified for reenlistment. The remaining 153 men had seemingly reached the end of the line. Apart from the fact that the decision of the court was deemed final and irrevocable, the soldiers' best ally, Senator Foraker, had been defeated in the 1908 Senate race, and one of their most formidable adversaries, William Howard Taft, had assumed the presidency.[58]

Though officially laid to rest, the Brownsville riot was not forgotten, particularly by African Americans. In November 1910 the first issue of The Crisis, the official organ of the recently established National Association for the Advancement of Colored People (NAACP) published an article by Moorfield Storey, a white liberal who served as chairman of the NAACP board. In the article Storey contrasted the Brownsville decision with treatment accorded a group of white soldiers in 1904. Storey noted that in that year between fifty and seventy-five white soldiers tried to break open a jail in Athens, Ohio, in order to release a comrade. During the attempt the soldiers killed one militiaman and wounded at least two others. Contending that, no matter how guilty a man was, "he was entitled to be defended by counsel," Secretary of War Taft assigned a representative of the War Department to defend the accused and arranged for an attorney from the Department of Justice to assist in the defense. The Secretary explained his active intervention on behalf of the soldiers: "An enlisted man is more or less a ward of the government, and if the government steps in merely to see that he

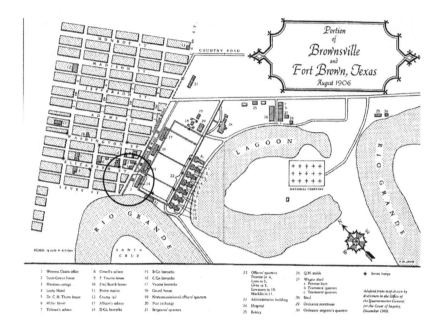

FIGURE 3.4. Fort Brown and adjacent area, with key buildings noted. The Louis Cowan House and Cowan's Alley are encircled. Adapted by Weaver, 1970 from map drawn by draftsmen in the Office of the Quartermaster General for the December 1909 Court of Inquiry.

is tried according to law, it seems to me that it is an exercise of discretion which the Government has."[59]

Despite losing his bid for reelection, Senator Foraker continued to advocate on behalf of the debarred soldiers, most notably in his 1916 autobiography which included three chapters on the Brownsville riot. Subsequent academic publications also addressed the issue, including some who compared the Brownsville incident with the Dreyfus affair.[60] One of these, *The Brownsville Raid: The Story of America's Black Dreyfus Affair*, by John D. Weaver, attracted the interest of Representative Augustus Hawkins, a black California Democrat. In 1971 Hawkins called on his colleagues in Congress to assist him in righting the "grievous wrong" committed against the soldiers. On September 28 of the following year, Secretary of the Army Robert F. Froehlke announced that the 167 enlisted men dismissed without honor in

FIGURE 3.5. The Louis Cowan House is to the right. Courtesy UT Brownsville Archives.

1906 were to be granted honorable discharges. Only two of them were still alive. One, Edward Warfield of Company B, was among those who had been permitted to reenlist by decision of the court of inquiry. The other, Dorsie W. Willis of Company D, received a $25,000 pension and was granted medical care at veterans' hospitals.

On December 27, 1972 the *New York Times* reported that Willis, "old, arthritic, and resentful," after his discharge had been reduced to working as a porter and shoeshine man. "That dishonorable discharge kept me from improving my station," Willis told the reporter. "Only God knows what it did to the others." He added bitterly, "None of us said anything, 'cause we didn't have anything to say. It was a frame-up straight through."

Dorsie Willis died August 24, 1977 at the age of ninety-one and was given a soldier's burial at Fort Snelling National Cemetery.

A Lack of Historical Commemoration

Fort Brown, the single most important site associated with the Brownsville Riot, has been severely impacted by modern

FIGURE 3.6.   Private Dorsie Willis receives a check for $25,000 and an honorable discharge from the U.S. Army, over sixty years after the Brownsville incident. Courtesy UT Brownsville archives.

development. Portions of the old fort are now occupied by the Brownsville Chamber of Commerce, the campus of the University of Texas at Brownsville, U.S. Customs, and the U.S. Citizenship and Immigration Service, among others.   However several historic structures and a portion of the original earthworks remain intact (Figures 3 and 4). In 1960 the fort was designated as a National Landmark with the following statement of significance:

> Established in April 1846 by Brig. Gen. Zachary Taylor, Fort Brown was under siege at the time of the battle of Palo Alto, and its siege was raised by the Americans' defeat of the Mexican army at Resaca de la Palma. Troops stationed here

fought the last battle of the Civil War; the fort was the center for troop activity during the Mexican bandit trouble of 1913-1917.

The 1966 listing for Fort Brown in the National Register of Historic Places highlights the following significance statement: "Throughout its history, Fort Brown contributed significantly to the defense of the nation, aiding greatly in the westward expansion of the United States."

These statements establish the national significance of the property as a series of events pertaining to the themes of military history and a particular interpretation of westward expansion. Neither narrative mentions the Brownsville Riot. Neither does the more recent work Fort Brown, Texas: A New Frontier by Sharyn Kane & Richard Keeton of the Southeast Archaeological Center of the National Park Service. However the 1906 Brownsville Raid also contributes to the national significance of the fort, not only in relation to military history, but also in terms of the themes of ethnic heritage, social history and politics. Inclusion of the Brownsville Riot in all statements and future studies would more accurately reflect the national significance of the site.

CHAPTER FOUR

A Brief Summary of the Houston Riot of 1917

The Houston Riot of 1917, also known as the Camp Logan Riot, Houston Race Riot, Camp Logan War, or Camp Logan Mutiny, was an uprising by members of the U.S. Army's all-black Third Battalion, 24th Infantry, against the Houston version of the Jim Crow system of white supremacy that existed throughout the southern states in the early part of the twentieth century.

The United States Congress declared war on Germany on April 4, 1917. Business leaders in Houston actively lobbied the War Department for military funding for the Bayou City. Funding for the construction of a new National Guard training facility named Camp Logan was announced in June of 1917. The black troops of the 24th were ordered to perform guard duty during the construction of Camp Logan, located on the outskirts of Houston, and arrived in the city from Columbus, New Mexico on July 28, 1917. Although the prospect of service near a city with a large black community was enticing, it was an assignment neither the black troops nor their white officers wanted, because of Texas' well-known reputation for racial violence and mistreatment of black soldiers.[1] The 1916 lynching of Jesse Washington in Waco, Texas, for instance, had been well publicized in the black press, and the 1899 incident at Rio Grande City and the 1906 incident at Brownsville had been part of the institutional memory of the regiment for years.[2]

The simple presence of uniformed and armed black soldiers in the Bayou City was enough to incite racial tension. Despite assurances by the Houston Chamber of Commerce to the War Department that the soldiers would be treated well, white Houstonians expected the soldiers to submit to the same discourtesies and insults of Jim Crow that the local black population had grown to begrudgingly accept. In Texas this meant the passive acceptance of verbal and psychological harassment, extreme segregation, insulting racial epithets, denial of voting rights and meaningful civic participation, substandard healthcare, public works, and education, plantation based convict labor camps, all-white juries, and Texas-sized demonstrations of racial violence: police brutality, indiscriminate killings, and lynchings.[3]

Upon receiving a rumor that a popular member of the battalion had been murdered by a member of the racist Houston police, on the evening of August 23, 1917 approximately 130 members of the 24th rioted. After raiding the camp's armory the soldiers marched three miles towards downtown Houston via the city's San Felipe neighborhood, also known as "Freedmenstown" or Fourth Ward. The riot lasted roughly three hours, and involved shootouts between the soldiers and members of the Houston police, members of other military units stationed in the city, and armed civilians. Twenty people died, four of them black, sixteen white. It is the only racially motivated riot in American history in which more white people died than black.[4]

118 members of the battalion were eventually arrested and charged with murder and mutiny by military authorities. A series of trials resulted in the conviction of 110 of the accused, in the largest military courts-martial in American history. Punishment ranged from sentences of two years to death. Of the 28 death sentences, 19 were ultimately carried out; the first 13 soldiers were hastily executed in the early morning of December 11, 1917 in San Antonio, Texas, before the cases could be reviewed and without family notification. After public outrage by the black community at this seeming miscarriage of justice, President Wilson ultimately commuted ten of the remaining death sentences to life in prison.[5]

The 1917 Houston Riot is one of the most important events in twentieth century African-American history as well as American military history. As a window into the tensions and injustices of American racism in the early twentieth century, the incident remains of central and enduring significance. It is of course also an important event in the history of Houston and of Texas. Inherently dramatic, the Shakespearean manner in which the tragedy unfolded also makes it a unique historical event that sheds important light into the difficulties faced by African-American soldiers in the first half of the twentieth century, and reinforces the consequences of the tragic unwillingness of the intransigent white supremacist power structure to learn the lessons of previous race "riots" of a similar nature.

Interpretations of what took place have had a complicated history and are an important part of the story. From the outset, black authors and scholars, particularly the black press, have tended to view the soldiers as martyrs and have placed blame for what happened with War Department officials, advocates at the Houston Chamber of Commerce, and on Texas Jim Crow in general. White writers over the years have demonstrated a greater tendency to blame the soldiers, either in whole or in part.

The former Camp Logan is now Houston's Memorial Park, with fine homes, wooded areas, and jogging trails.

CHAPTER FIVE

The Houston Riot of 1917

The City of Houston

Founded in 1836 by two land speculators from New York and named for Texas revolutionary hero Sam Houston, the city of Houston in 1917 was a typical southern hustle and bustle cotton port that had supplanted Texas' largest and most important nineteenth century port city, Galveston, which was destroyed by the great hurricane of 1900. The fast growing city had a population of about 130,000 in 1917, about 25 percent of whom were black and segregated.[1]

As with nineteenth century Galveston, the chief driver of Houston's economy was cotton. Over sixty firms, employing over ten thousand workers, exported more than 3 million bales of cotton from the Bayou City per year, making Houston the largest inland cotton port in the world. The city's progressive political and economic policies during this period facilitated even further growth; the Houston Ship Channel opened in 1914, making Houston a deepwater port, and aggressive post Civil War railroad construction further contributed to the city's growth and lively reputation. City leaders also pursued robust public works strategies, at least in white areas of town. For instance in 1915 the city had almost 196 miles of paved streets and implemented significant drainage infrastructure, an important civic responsibility in a sub-tropical swamp city like Houston that is subject to flooding.[2]

The city's rise in population matched its rapid economic growth. Blacks from rural Texas and Louisiana flocked to Houston in search of jobs. They settled in neighborhoods such as Fourth Ward or "Freedmentown," the city's original post Civil War Negro settlement located on the west side of the city, and found work on the docks as cotton and lumber stevedores, while black women found work as domestics, seamstresses or other service employment. The discovery of oil and the completion of the area's first oil refinery in 1918 were further stimuli to the city's political economy.

There were some unique features to segregation in early twentieth century Houston. Unlike many African Americans living in eastern and midwestern cities who were confined to urban ghettoes, Houston's African American community enjoyed a semi-rural existence. The city's population, though growing rapidly, was still relatively small, land was plentiful, real estate lot sizes were large, and population densities were low. "Many blacks recalled the small town atmosphere of black neighborhoods as late as the 1930s and early 1940s."[3]

Initially organized by wards, the city's political system similarly underwent rapid change. Aldermen began to be elected at large in a modified commission form of government in 1905. In February 1917 a city council member and former tax commissioner named Joseph Jay Pastoriza was elected mayor of Houston, despite strong opposition from Houston's business community. Running as a reformer, Pastoriza initiated investigations of two of the city's most significant institutions, the Houston Lighting and Power Company and the Houston Police Department. The investigation of the police was particularly important, especially to the city's black population, which held most of the the police department in contempt, although Pastoriza was mostly responding to the city's "respectable" white population which wanted prostitution, gambling, alcohol, and vice controlled if not eliminated. Unfortunately Pastoriza was never able to carry out his investigations or reforms. He died on July 9, 1917, shortly before the arrival of the black troops of the Twenty-fourth Infantry. The Mayor pro tem of Houston temporarily assumed the duties of mayor until a special election could be held.

The Houston Police Department

The overt racism of the Houston police department was a matter of record. For instance in a moment of "slave patrol" nostalgia, Ben S. Davidson, the hand picked superintendent of police installed by previous Houston mayor Ben Campbell, in 1915 requested "a pack of bloodhounds" in order to "exert a moral effect...especially among the negro race." The plantation style racism exhibited by the police superintendent was deeply institutionalized within the police force, which in 1917 consisted of 159 men, only two of which were black and who exclusively patrolled black neighborhoods (a black police officer could not arrest white offenders, and faced instant dismissal if white citizens complained). The racism of the police was reflective of the Houston citizenry at large, one of whom observed that "our policemen have to beat the niggers when they are insolent....you can't expect them to let a nigger curse them."[4]

The stock-in-trade of the Houston police force was fear. By terrorizing the black population of the city with arbitrary violence or its ever-present possibility, white police officers engaged in patterns of sadism with deep roots in the institution of slavery. For example "one policeman pointed a pistol at the head of a black iceman because he was not as punctual in making his delivery as the lawman thought he should have been" and then pulled the trigger.[5] The gun was not loaded, but that mattered little to the frightened ice block deliverer when he heard the pistol hammer drop. False arrests, mysterious shootings, and unannounced day or night house entries were also facts of life in black neighborhoods. These behaviors were not individual acts of prejudice, they reflected deeply ingrained attitudes within the Houston police department: "City detective Jim Fife told an investigating body that firing three shots 'in the ground thinking he would stop' was standard police procedure" with negro suspects.[6]

White dissatisfaction with the lack of professionalism of the Houston police force also had a sizable foundation. Wild West style gunplay on the city's streets lasted well into the twentieth century; as recently as 1911 two policemen settled a personal grudge by engaging in a pistol duel on Main Street, and armed posses of "bad men" would periodically terrorize the town by engaging in indiscriminate shooting and intimidation of downtown pedestrians.[7]   White citizens also bemoaned the police's active and passive support for after hours drinking and misbehavior, particularly in the city's noted vice district known as "the reservation," which was located in a ten block portion of Fourth Ward, the city's oldest black neighborhood.

In his short term as mayor, Pastoriza undertook a variety of initiatives in order to reform the police force. He replaced the existing police chief Ben Davidson with the Superintendent of Parks, Clarence L. Brock and undertook a series of reforms designed to increase police pride and good order and discipline in the force. For the first time, patrol officers were subject to daily inspection and were expected to project a neat appearance. Training expectations also increased, and Brock's inspector of police Ormond Paget had the officers perform various training maneuvers such as close order drill. The reforms were not received well; several senior police officers openly opposed Chief Brock and scoffed at his reorganization and improvement efforts. Political turmoil ensued, and the dissatisfied police officers conspired with their former chief Ben Davidson to have the new police superintendent twice indicted by a Harris County grand jury for false imprisonment. Alongside the sudden death of the mayor, this severely undermined Brock's authority and reform efforts, and created a climate where the police rank and file behaved in a manner befitting the status quo ante of tolerance for prostitution, gambling, drinking, vice and violence.

Disgusted by the political theater and gamesmanship being played by the city's politicians, a group of reform minded Houston citizens organized themselves into a church based ministerial alliance and formed a "committee of 100" dedicated to shutting down the reservation and elevating the city's frontier reputation. The prohibitionist group hired a private investigator known as "Mr. Chesterfield" who produced a damning report quantifying the degree of prostitution and gambling taking place in the city, and naming the landlords and owners of the private residences where the illegal activities were taking place. "The names of these prominent Houstonians were never made public, but the threat of exposure was enough to drive them to cover."[8] Police chief Brock eventually endorsed their efforts.[9]

The summer 1917 closure of the reservation exacerbated a bad situation. Police brutality incidents rose to an all time high as black women were reduced to streetwalking, unlike white prostitutes, who had the option of moving their businesses to quieter parts of town. The effort by moral reformers to turn Harris County dry similarly had a negative effect on the black population; the bootleggers arrested for violating the liquor laws were usually black, even though whites were the greater offenders.[10] By almost exclusively concentrating their efforts to combat gambling, alcohol, and street crime on the black community, the Houston police compiled an impressive list of arrests, satisfying the moralists without unduly upsetting the rest of the white community, some of whom continued to clandestinely benefit from the same criminal activities for which blacks were being brutally mistreated.

The Push for Camp Logan and Ellington Field

The declaration of war against Germany was greeted with enthusiasm by most Houstonians. The contents of the Zimmerman telegram—in which Germany offered to assist Mexico in "reconquer[ing]" its lost territories, including Texas—found a particularly enkindled audience in the Bayou City, the namesake of the "hero" of San Jacinto, Sam Houston.[11] Lobbying for wartime spending began almost immediately. "By the late spring of 1917 no fewer than half a dozen prominent Houstonians were in Washington, D.C. seeking favors for themselves or promoting the city's interests before various federal agencies."[12]   Representatives of the chamber of commerce, particularly the city's oil, cotton, and lumber industries used their clout within the democratic party and with the Wilson administration to push for wartime appropriations. They stressed Houston's favorable climate, its geographic proximity to strategic locations such as the new Panama Canal, and also offered the War Department an in-kind contribution of fifteen thousand acres of land, accompanied by the promise that the real estate's infrastructure would be developed at local expense.

After conducting a brief study, the War Department eventually decided to build a national guard training facility named Camp Logan along the western outskirts of the city and a new Army Air facility named Ellington Field about eighteen miles east of the city.

The local business community was elated, although some were disappointed that the camp would only be a temporary training facility. One leader argued that the projects were the "greatest prize" in the city's history with the exception of the ship channel.[13]   In a further boost to the local economy, a Houston construction firm was awarded the contract to build Camp Logan. Newspapers, politicians, business, and civic leaders warmly saluted the expected two million dollar monthly boost to the local economy, although lobbying efforts persisted, in the hope of upgrading Camp Logan into a permanent military base.

Construction began in earnest on July 25, 1917 and rapidly picked up speed. An initial crew of 250 workmen set about constructing over 700 buildings and about ten miles of roadbeds, with the crew growing to a size of over 4,000 by the end of August.

In a move that surprised and stunned white Houstonians, the War Department announced that it was sending Negro troops to guard federal property during the construction of Camp Logan. The response of the chamber of commerce was to author a polite letter to military authorities in San Antonio informing them of the inappropriateness of such a decision and suggesting that it might be better to utilize the services of the Texas National Guard, shortly to be mobilized. These developments placed the city's lobbyists in a difficult position; their efforts to secure permanent status for Camp Logan as a military base, was in conflict with the War Department's decision to station black troops there. In the end the chamber of commerce relented when it was informed by War Department officials that only black troops were available and that they would only be in Houston for seven weeks. James George, the chamber of commerce secretary promised Maj. James Parker, Southern department commander that "...[the] negro soldiers....will be properly received and....their comfort will be given due consideration." He added, however, a potential disclaimer: "You need anticipate no trouble as long as they comport themselves as soldiers should."[14]

Given the circumstances, the War Department's claim to City of Houston officials that the black troops were the only ones available at the time was not truthful. The decision to station black troops in southern locales was in reality more about race than about troop availability. In keeping with prevailing racial attitudes of the era, the Wilson administration and Secretary of War Newton D. Baker resisted sending black troops to fight on the front lines in World War I, despite the exemplary combat track record of the Buffalo Soldier regiments.[15] Consequently, black members of the regular army needed to be stationed somewhere in support of the war effort, and the War Department made the executive decision to station them in southern locations over the strenuous objections of white southerners and their political leaders. Members of the 24th Infantry Regiment were not elated over being suddenly reduced from the position of a fighting force to that of a guard detail. Barred from service in the Marine Corps, permitted to serve in the Navy only in the most menial jobs, and forbidden from service in the Army aviation corps, blacks who wanted to fight in the Great War as officers or aviators largely did so in foreign militaries. One noteworthy example is Eugene J. Bullard, the first

African-American fighter pilot, who fought in the war on behalf of France.[16]

The Twenty-fourth Infantry in Houston

Companies I, K, L, and M of the Twenty-fourth infantry moved into temporary quarters about one half mile east of Camp Logan on July 28, 1917. The detachment consisted of 645 enlisted men and seven officers under the command of Lieutenant Colonel William Newman. At the time it was ordered to Houston the Third Battalion had been experiencing considerable personnel challenges. Fifty new recruits had recently joined the ranks, and twenty-five of its most experienced noncommissioned officers had been transferred to the Fort Des Moines Training Camp for Colored Officers in Iowa, a camp established by the War Department in response to longstanding black activist calls for an increase in Negro officers.[17]

The removal of such a large segment of the battalion's senior enlisted leadership created an unstable environment that would prove to have dire consequences. The newly appointed NCO's did not have sufficient time to establish their authority and to earn the troops' respect. The position of First Sergeant was particularly important; as the senior enlisted liaison between the battalion's white officers and the rank and file, the holder of that position needed to be in possession of excellent human relations skills in order to function effectively within a Jim Crow environment.[18]

The Third Battalion's officers were not the best the army had to offer, and there were too few of them. The unit arrived in Houston with less than half of the sixteen commissioned officers assigned to it, and two of the companies were commanded by first lieutenants instead of captains. There were no second lieutenants, the only rank technically available to black regular army officers, had these existed.

In addition to Colonel Newman, who took command of the Third Battalion on the day it left for Houston, the remaining officers included Captain Haig Shekerjian, the only officer of Armenian descent to serve in the U.S. Army, as well as Capt. Kneeland S. Snow, I Company commander, Capt. W.H. Reisinger, Jr., K Company commander, First Lieutenant Bartlett James of Company L, and First Lieutenant Lindsey McDonald Silvester of Company M. As a group the officers were at best average; with the exception of when they had duties to perform, they were usually out in town enjoying the benefits of wearing an officer's uniform in a city anxious to please the military. The officers spent considerable amounts of time in Houston saloons, and Captain Snow took particular interest in working on his golf game with a civilian grocery supplier who soon acquired most of the contracts for supplying the camp. A married man, he also took the time to amuse himself with women friends.[19]

Upon learning that the battalion would be stationed in Houston, Col. Newman tried to get the order revoked. In a letter to military authorities in San Antonio he wrote:

> I had already had an unfortunate experience when I was in command of two companies of the 24th infantry at Del Rio, Texas, in April 1916, when a colored soldier was killed by a [Texas] ranger for no other reason than that he was a colored man; that it angered Texans to see colored men in the uniform of a soldier.

Newman's concerns and first-hand experience had good foundation. The simple appearance of blacks in uniform, armed or not, was sufficient to activate white racial hatred. Blacks were lynched in Mississippi and Georgia for appearing on the street in uniform, and members of the Twenty-fourth were quite aware of Texas' well deserved reputation for lynchings and other forms of racial violence.[20] The death of Booker T. Washington, the best-known black leader famous for his accommodationist politics also influenced the mindset of the troops, many of whom were avid readers of the NAACP's organ The Crisis, edited by W.E.B. Du

Bois.[21]   Newman was also acting upon concerns voiced by his men.   For instance Cecil Green, a black sergeant with the battalion, later stated that the troops "expected trouble in Houston from [white] mobs" from the beginning.[22]

War department officials denied Newman's request and informed him of the Houston chamber of commerce's promises that the soldiers would be treated well.

The Third Battalion set up camp near the western edge of Houston; July 28, 1917 was a Saturday, and the presence of black troops in the city gathered attention.   Colonel Newman attempted to manage the situation by undertaking efforts to minimize interaction between white Houstonians and the troops. He forbad most of his men from visiting the city, instead allowing black Houstonians the privilege of visiting the camp between 1:00 p.m. and 10:45 p.m., a lax policy that was later said to have been a contributing factor to the riot.   Only senior personnel and highly disciplined troops received routine passes into town.   Lastly, in order to placate white fears of armed black troops he disarmed his own men; not even military police were allowed to have weapons while in the city, an emasculating order that did not endear Newman to his already skeptical troops and which made the job of his military police officers difficult if not impossible.

The soldiers did find ways to stay entertained.   Enterprising businesspeople near the location of the camp set up eating establishments and recreational facilities, most of which were cheerfully patronized by the troops.   One establishment in particular, known as "the dance hall" was located about 150 yards west of the camp and became a favored hangout spot for the troops.

The Lead-up to the Riot

Colonel Newman's efforts to limit interactions between his soldiers and civilians seemed to be working.   When he left

Houston for his new duty station on August 20, the local white newspapers generously praised Newman for his time in the city and the discipline displayed by his troops.

But beneath this surface veneer of grudging collegiality simmered a slumbering volcano. For weeks tempers had flared between the black soldiers guarding the construction of Camp Logan and the white workmen. The laborers' repeated and vigorous use of the epithet "Nigger" enraged the soldiers, as did signs of Jim Crow such as racially labeled drinking containers. The soldiers who did enter town also took exception to the segregation of the city's streetcars and the discourteous manner in which the car operators enforced those regulations. According to the questionable post-riot testimony of some streetcar conductors, on at least two occasions black soldiers ripped the "colored" signs from the streetcars and either tossed them out the window or kept them as souvenirs.[23] Other streetcar incidents involved platoons of soldiers anxious to return to camp for their 11:00 p.m. bed check overflowing the colored section of the car and being told to get off by the white conductor when they started utilizing the less than full white section.

An incident in Waco involving the First Battalion of the Twenty-fourth also served to heighten tensions in Houston. On the evening of Sunday July 29, 1917, after experiencing the customary Jim Crow treatment in restaurants, accommodations, restaurants, saloons, and movie houses, several members of the battalion got into fights with members of the Waco police in a segregated restaurant where one of the battalion members had ripped down a "colored only" sign. Around midnight thirteen armed members of the battalion left camp with the intention of confronting the Waco police. A shootout ensued but was quelled when the soldiers realized that the figures they were shooting at in the dark were not Waco policemen but members of a provost guard sent to retrieve them. Order was subsequently re-established. They key factor in the handling of this incident is that the Waco police department did not exacerbate the situation and deferred to the military's handling of the matter.[24]

The streetcar incidents and the Waco disturbance frightened both civil and military authorities in Houston and led to meeting between Col. Newman and David Daly, traffic manager for the Houston Electric Company, and Ben Davidson, the former police chief, now representing the chamber of commerce. A later meeting with the new chief of police, Clarence Brock was also held. Agreements were concluded to deal with the situation, including the running of more streetcar lines at certain times, as well as the stationing of more military police in the San Felipe District, also known as Fourth Ward or Freedmantown, a location considered a trouble spot by the police.[25] Chief Brock also agreed to instruct his officers to cooperate fully with the disarmed provost guards.

Given the tenuousness of his political position as police chief, Brock was in no position to make such a promise, and Newman never actually confirmed that the Houston police got the message. It is not clear whether Brock actually gave the order, but even if he did it was ignored. In hindsight it seems clear that no amount of concessions on the part of Newman could have conciliated the police rank and file, who expected the soldiers, including their military police units, to behave like Houston civilians by passively accepting subjugation and maltreatment. In short, the police thought the federal uniform of the soldiers irrelevant and treated them like any other "niggers." In the end, Newman's numerous efforts to conciliate the intransigent Jim Crow system of Houston did not work and placed his disarmed —and thus defenseless—troops at the mercy of racist law enforcement thugs.

The weeks leading up to the riot were also characterized by numerous altercations between the soldiers and the Camp Logan construction team's white workforce. The initial verbal exchanges were tense but tolerable, but as the weeks wore on outright physical altercation seemed ineluctable. The white workers expected the soldiers to exercise deference in accordance with southern custom, but the soldiers instead informed the workers, initially politely and professionally, that they resented being called niggers and preferred to be referred to as colored men. The response of the white carpenters and pipe-fitters was to engage in threatening insults[26] and to complain about the insolence of the soldiers. By mid-August some of the carpenters quit because they could see that "just as plain as anything that trouble was coming."[27]

Too busy having a good time, the Twenty-fourth infantry's officers lacked the powers of perception to understand the growing volatility of the situation. Swamped by the increasing volume of complaints from white workmen—many of them frivolous—and other white Houstonians about the "insolent" negro soldiers, they eventually grew frustrated at both sides and stopped investigating complaints. Unsympathetic, selfish, and living in a bubble divorced from the realities their soldiers were experiencing, the officers did not understand why the men could not behave themselves by simply adjusting themselves to the Jim Crow customs of their new duty station. As a consequence "most of the soldiers considered the white officers to be incapable of judging their conduct impartially. Their reluctance to report instances of abuse misled the officers into thinking that the men were more content with conditions in Houston than they actually were."[28] When violence finally came, the officers were taken completely by surprise.

In some respects the group that found the presence of Negro troops in Houston most offensive of all were members of the newly mobilized Fifth Infantry of the Texas National Guard. The commander of the Texas guard and also a longtime resident of Houston (where he worked as a railroad executive), Brigadier General John A. Hulen, summed up the prevailing attitude about the uppity negroes of the Twenty-fourth fairly well when he stated that the negro soldiers "seemed to think that they had greater privileges than other negroes in the community."[29] Mustered into federal service on August 5, 1917, the twelve-hundred guard soldiers were temporarily housed in the downtown area of Houston while awaiting orders to Camp Bowie in Fort Worth. Many of the members of the Texas guard units were from the East Texas plantation belt (e.g. Trinity and Polk counties) and found the presence of uniformed black troops in Houston to be an almost unfathomable culture shock. Verbal insults between members of the Twenty-fourth and the guardsmen happened almost every time they encountered one another on the street. Col. Newman and the guard commander Col. John S. Hoover conferred regularly, with Newman taking the customary steps to keep his black troops away from white guardsmen as much as possible.

The conflict between the members of the Twenty-fourth and these forces can be explained simply: the black soldiers insisted upon being treated as equals and with the respect due of highly decorated service members wearing the uniform of the United States. They also actively asserted their unwillingness to accept the racial attitudes and treatment of white Houstonians. This behavior was perceived by white Houstonians as impertinent and as a contagion that could potentially infect the black civilian population of Houston.[30]

The Riot

The events that would lead to violent confrontation between the Twenty-fourth and the Houston police began on the morning of August 23, 1917, a time of stifling humidity levels and routine high temperatures well in excess of one-hundred degrees Fahrenheit. Two mounted Houston police officers, Lee Sparks and Rufus Daniels, broke up a dice game involving black teenagers and during the chase that ensued shot at them and burst into an adjoining house seeking their whereabouts. The home belonged to Mrs. Sara Travers, a mother of five, who was busy ironing clothes and resented the home invasion. Not expecting company, she was only partly dressed. After a brief altercation, the officers arrested Mrs. Travers and dragged her into the street in front of her home. Before being thrown into the street she begged the officers to be allowed to put on some clothes. Sparks replied that she would be taken as she was, even if naked. Travers then grabbed her baby and asked Sparks to let her take the infant with her. Sparks took the baby from her hands and threw it down on the sidewalk. Mrs. Travers's began crying and shouting, and begged to know why she was being arrested; others noticed the fracas and a crowd began to gather in front of her house. Sparks later testified that she was being arrested for "abusive language."[31]

Private Alonzo Edwards of Company L was in the crowd and heard Mrs. Travers' screams. He walked up to Sparks and Edwards to inquire about what was going on. Annoyed that a black soldier would dare question his police procedure, Sparks, one of the Houston police department's more prominent racists and under investigation for a previous excessive force incident, pistol whipped Edwards and arrested him alongside Travers. The charge against Edwards was "interfering" with an arrest.

Later that afternoon Corporal Charles Baltimore, a military policeman from Company I approached Sparks and Daniels near the arrest scene and inquired about Edwards. Baltimore, a highly regarded soldier, was the provost guard on duty. Similarly incensed, Sparks drew his pistol and proceeded to assault Corporal Baltimore, who fled and was shot at by Sparks several times. Baltimore, who was hiding under a bed in a local home, was eventually captured by the police and after being roughed up some more was brought to the police station. "Sparks later claimed that he attacked Baltimore in response to the man's abusive language and that he fired the shots into the ground. Witnesses refuted the statements. A resident of the neighborhood insisted that the officer 'shot right at him...into a street full of women and children.'"[32]

Following the Baltimore incident, rumors quickly spread that he had been killed and that a white mob was planning an attack upon Camp Logan. Members of the Twenty-fourth, clearly irate and "excited and talking to one another," began to seriously think about taking matters into their own hands.

Finally realizing that his men were at the end of their rope and on the verge of mutiny, Major Kneeland Snow, who had relieved Newman as battalion commander on August 20th, proceeded to Houston police headquarters accompanied by Captain Haig Shekerjian, his chief of military police.   There they found Baltimore, severely beaten and wounded, but alive.   During a meeting with police chief Clarence Brock, Snow explained that Baltimore was simply doing his duty as a military policeman by questioning Sparks about Edwards. Brock responded by releasing Baltimore back to military custody and by promising to suspend Sparks without pay for his unwarranted attack.[33]

Aware of Corporal Baltimore's popularity with the soldiers, Snow assembled his senior enlisted leadership and briefed them about the situation. In order to diffuse the rumor that Baltimore had been killed, he also briefly presented the corporal before his noncommissioned officers and instructed them to relay the information to the troops, along with Brock's promises. Snow also cancelled passes for the night, postponing a watermelon party that had been scheduled for Emancipation Park, and posted three additional camp guards, raising the total to six. Convinced that these measures were adequate to handle the situation, Snow then foolishly made preparations to leave the camp for the evening, something he had been accustomed to doing during his Houston stay.

Tensions in the camp remained high, however, because many of the soldiers continued to believe that an armed white mob was coming to attack them. Sometime between eight and nine o'clock in the evening a shout from Private Frank Johnson pierced the darkness: "Get your guns men! The white mob is coming! Frustrated and afraid, some of the disarmed soldiers began to take matters into their own hands and proceeded to their tents and to the camp armory to obtain weapons and ammunition. In the chaos that ensued, shots began to be fired into the night against perceived invaders, and eventually approximately 100 soldiers formed a column and began marching in the direction of downtown Houston to seek revenge upon the Houston police officers responsible for the beatings of Private Edwards and Corporal Baltimore.

The column began to divide into several groups of armed soldiers and proceeded easterly and northerly toward downtown Houston. Although they had marched towards the city with the intent of avenging themselves on the police, the soldiers also fired on others. Once in the city, the mutineers fought a series of skirmishes with the police and their deputies before disbanding and slipping back out of town. In the two hours that the riot lasted, 15 whites, including four Houston policemen, Daniels among them, were killed and 12 others seriously wounded. Four soldiers died. The only serious property damage took place when white Houstonians looted stores in search of firearms for protection. No black Houstonians took part in the riot.

Once the melee began, both the military and civilian leadership were exposed as inept. Flailing about for control of his men, Major Snow freely acknowledged that they "paid no attention to me whatsoever" and instead of taking command of the situation he lost his composure and issued fumbling and unclear directives in multiple directions. A Texas guardsman who wrote down Snow's comments when the Major telephoned former police chief Ben Davidson in a state of panic asserted that "I remember distinctly Major Snow's inability to direct his thought with clearness."[34] Other witnesses also commented on Snow's diminished mental state and unfitness for command.[35]

Local law enforcement matched Snow's incompetence. Chief Brock and Sheriff Frank Hammond made no provisions for increased security, despite their knowledge of the rapidly escalating situation. Numerous citizens called in between 8:30 and 9:30 p.m. with reports of armed soldiers on the streets, yet Hammond left town and Brock retired early.[36] In one of his last acts before his impeachment on August 25, 1917, Texas governor James E. Ferguson declared martial law, and Texas national guard troops from Galveston and San Antonio were dispatched. A local posse of 250 citizen deputies was hastily organized by Sheriff Hammond as well. By dawn the next morning the city's streets were calm.

The Aftermath

Simultaneous military and civilian investigations were undertaken. Many Houstonians wanted the soldiers brought to trial in a Houston courtroom and to face local punishment, but the army asserted jurisdiction and quickly removed the soldiers back to Camp Furlong in Columbus, New Mexico and eventually to Fort Bliss in El Paso. Unable to obtain a grand jury indictment, the interim Houston mayor ultimately appointed a seven member panel to conduct a civilian investigation of the incident. "Unsurprisingly, after several days of testimony, the board of inquiry placed most of the guilt on the army. It censured Chief Brock's ineptitude and Officer Sparks's misconduct in striking Baltimore, but concluded that the riot would have occurred in any event."[37] The civilian report was well received by the Houston establishment. It laid blame on the army for its lack of proper discipline of its Negro troops and exonerated the city from blame: "There was no provocation" stated a *Houston Post* editorial.[38]

The prevailing white sentiment about the causes of the conflagration was summed up by Dr. W.S. Lockhart, the pastor of South End Christian Church. At a funeral sermon for police officer Ira D. Raney, who was killed by the rioting soldiers, Lockhart flatly rejected the idea that "race troubles" in Houston could have been a factor. "The real facts" declared the pastor, "were that the mutiny was due to just two causes—vice and booze." "It was simply a case of a bunch of bad niggers dressed up in a uniform, given a little authority and put under very lax discipline, who, under the influence of women and booze, perpetrated this murderous crime against the army and the city of Houston."[39]

Shortly after the incident the NAACP sent an investigator from New York to appreciate the situation. Martha Gruening, the association's reporter, found a city where whites had assigned proper blame and largely made up their mind and where blacks were quietly outraged or afraid. "In contrast to white citizens whose conversation dwelled upon the riot's tragic results, blacks primarily talked about the circumstances that had caused the unfortunate occurrence."[40] Her investigation revealed that the colored population of Houston largely felt that the disarming of the soldiers was a key factor in causing the riot. One interviewee declared that "if Corporal Baltimore had been armed, they would never have dared to set upon him and we should not have had a riot." He went on to note, "you may have observed....that Southerners do not like to fight Negroes on equal terms." She also made sure to note that the incidents with Private Edwards and Corporal Baltimore were not the first incidents of their kind:

> A few days before a Negro had been beaten on a car by city detective Ed Stoermer, who according to his own testimony before the Citizens Investigating Committee, cleared the car of its white passengers, telling them that "he might have to kill the nigger." I was reliably informed that on another occasion two colored soldiers were brutally beaten up by city detectives who boarded the car in which they sat from a Ford machine; that this machine drew up alongside of the car which was halted by the conductor long enough for the beating to take place, after which the detectives again got into the car and drove off.[41]

Regarding direct testimony about other police brutality incidents, one of Gruening's interviewees flatly declared that "there's a lot more I could say, only I'm afeard." Barely a week after the riot Sparks shot an unarmed army draftee named Williams in the back during a dice game on Dallas Avenue; the man later died.   Free on bond, not suspended pending investigation, and certainly not apt to be convicted of murder by an all-white jury, about a week after the riot he

> entered the house of a respectable colored physician on Robbin Avenue early in the morning while the latter was in his bath and his wife partly dressed, on the pretext of looking for a fugitive, insulted and bullied them both when they protested, and threatened them with a drawn gun. On the same day he threatened a colored woman that he would "blow her damned head off" because he thought she had laughed at him. It was in pursuit of this woman that he entered several colored houses in this block, threatening and cursing the colored people.[42]

Gruening's NAACP investigation concluded that the police were to blame for the beginning of the riot, with the disarming of the soldiers and the supposed lax discipline at Camp Logan as underlying factors.[43]

The Houston riot was an event of national significance, and nothing since the Brownsville raid of 1906 had brought so much notoriety to black soldiers of the regular army.   1917 saw a number of racial incidents take place across the country, but of these only the East St. Louis riot was comparable in size and violence to the Houston affray.   Two significant differences, however, distinguish the Houston Riot from the others: it was the first riot in which more whites were killed than blacks, and it was one of the few riots that did not involve black civilians.[44]

Disgruntled that the soldiers would not face a criminal probe in Harris County, Houston city leaders placed pressure on the army to seek as harsh a verdict as possible. The lessons of the 1906 Brownsville Riot had been learned; there was not going to be another conspiracy of silence.   The city blamed the army, and the army blamed the soldiers. After a series of investigations, a series of courts-martial were undertaken by the army, and from the outset it became clear that the purpose of the trials was not to seek justice but to assign blame.

The trials took place between November, 1917 and March, 1918. The first trial, *U.S. vs. Sgt. William C. Nesbit et al.* charged sixty-three defendants with mutiny, murder, and felonious assault. The second trial, *U.S. v. Cpl. John Washington et al.* convened in December to judge fifteen members of the guard who abandoned their posts, resulting in the shooting death of jitney driver E.M. Jones. The third trial, *U.S. v. Cpl. Robert Tillman et al.* began on February 18 and was largely based on additional evidence gathered during the previous two trials, which incriminated forty additional battalion members.[45] Although the army charged 118 men with participation in the mutiny and riot, the actual number can never be determined, partly because of the officers' inability to take a proper roll call during the time the rioters were absent. The scene that evening was a confused mess; in addition to the rioting soldiers, some soldiers formed a picket line in anticipation of of an attack by a white mob, others hid once the shooting started. As a result the army based its case primarily on the testimony of several junior enlisted men who confessed to participating in the mutiny and riot in exchange for immunity or prosecutorial leniency.[46] Trial records indicate that these men were frightened into testifying against their fellow soldiers and that they were given questions at trial that were worded to elicit a preconceived response, particularly the testimony of Cleda Love of I Company, a twenty-year old recruit with less than six months of military service.[47]

The accused were defended by a single defense counsel in all three trials, Maj. Harry H. Grier. Grier was a career infantry officer, not a licensed attorney, although he had extensive experience working with black troops. The chief reason he seems to have been assigned to defend the accused soldiers of the Twenty-fourth is that he was available. The lead prosecution team consisted of Col. John A. Hull, judge advocate general of the Central Department in Chicago, assisted by Maj. Dudley V. Sutphin, a reserve officer who was a member of a prominent

Cincinnati law firm where he had distinguished himself as a corporate lawyer and superior court judge.[48] Major Grier had a difficult assignment; General John Wilson Ruckman, the new head of the Southern Department, only gave Grier two weeks to prepare for trial, whereas the prosecution was given over two months to prepare its strategy.[49] It was obvious that Grier lacked the resources and skills necessary to mount an adequate defense. Regrettably, he did not request a trial postponement or additional resources for his clients. He had all 63 defendants in the first trial enter "not guilty" pleas.[50]

Hull's trial strategy rested upon establishing that the entire mutiny and riot was premeditated, with certain soldiers, particularly Sgt. Vida Henry, among the ringleaders. One of his early witnesses to this effect was Maj. Kneeland Snow, who testified that the soldiers had grabbed their weapons "because they had a job to do" not because they were in fear of a white mob.[51] The prosecution in all three trials put forth the notion of collective responsibility for the mutiny and riot, under the theory that certain conspirators should not escape punishment because of the state's inability to identify the identity of specific individuals. Maj. Grier's defense strategy primarily relied on attempting to defend the accused soldiers as individuals instead of as a group. He acknowledged that some members of the battalion were culpable, but that they were not as numerous as the prosecution claimed, and that they were led astray by the true leaders of the riot, Sgt. Henry chief among them.

Maj. Grier's strategy failed. On the morning of Thursday, November 29, 1917 the court handed down its decision in the first trial: Fifty-four of the sixty-three defendants were found guilty of all charges, four were found guilty of willful disobeyance of a lawful order for leaving camp, and five were acquitted. The defendants were then excused from the court while the court president announced the sentences. Thirteen of the fifty-four would be "hung by the neck until dead," with the remaining 41 soldiers sentenced to life at hard labor. The remaining four received shorter prison sentences.

Five of the thirteen—Nesbit, Baltimore, Larmon Brown, James Wheatley, and Jesse Moore—were noncommissioned officers. The other eight were Privates Pat McWhorter, Ira B. Davis, James Divins, William Breckenridge, Thomas C. Hawkins, Carlos Snodgrass, Frank Johnson, and Risley Young. All but McWhorter were members of I Company.[52] At the trial the defendants had specifically requested a firing squad in the event any death sentences were handed down, but the court-martial elected to hand down the more forceful (and unusual) punishment of death by hanging. Ironically Corporal Baltimore, whose beating allegedly sparked the riot, was among those who were convicted, though the Houston civilian board found him innocent.

The condemned men were not informed of their punishment until December 9. In the early morning of December 11, 1917 they were awakened and taken by truck to a stand of mesquite on the banks of Salado Creek at the edge of Camp Travis, an army training facility attached to Fort Sam Houston, where they were hanged in secret, without notification to the Secretary of War or the President, or to the respective families. The scaffolding used to hang the soldiers was quickly dismantled and burned, and the men were placed in coffins marked only with metal plaques numbered 1 to 13. The startled press was notified of the executions at nine o' clock in the morning, December 11.[53]

White public reaction was as expected. The white press generally applauded the verdicts and the method of execution. Black reaction, too, was as expected, almost one hundred percent negative. Shortly after the riot, in the October, 1917 *Crisis* magazine, W.E.B. Du Bois opined "Here at last, at Houston is a change: here at last white folk died...perhaps as innocent as the thousands of Negroes done to death in the last two centuries...They [the soldiers] were disciplined men who said —'this is enough: we'll stand no more."[54] In another early reaction to the mutiny and riot, the *Baltimore Afro-American* editorialized that "A Negro in military uniform is as exasperating to the average Texan as is the flaunting of a red flag in the face of an enraged bull," and in a jab at President Wilson, whose efforts at stirring up a reluctant nation to continue to support the U.S. war effort in Europe, the editor said:

President Wilson made a trenchant statement in a speech in Philadelphia to the effect that "A man may be too proud to fight." With equal force it may be said that man may be too manly to continually submit to extreme brutal treatment. Even the patient ox may be goaded to desperation.[55]

The post-execution black reaction was somber and poetic. The *New York Age* declared "Strict justice has been done, but full justice has not been done....And so sure as there is a God in heaven, at some time and in some way full justice will be done."[56] The January 1918 edition of *The Crisis* contains a picture, one of the few available, of the trial shot by W.C. Lloyd. Du Bois, in a section of the magazine simply titled "Thirteen" wrote:

They have gone to their death. Thirteen young, strong men; soldiers who have fought for a country which never was wholly theirs; men born to suffer ridicule, injustice, and, at last, death itself. They broke the law. Against their punishment, if it was legal, we cannot protest. But we can protest and we do protest against the shameful treatment which these men and which we, their brothers, receive all our lives, and which our fathers received, and our children await; and above all we raise our clenched hands against the hundreds of thousands of white murderers, rapists, and scoundrels who have oppressed, killed, ruined, robbed, and debased their black fellow men and fellow women, and yet, today, walk scot-free, unwhipped of justice, uncondemned by millions of their white fellow citizens, and unrebuked by the President of the United States.[57]

Even moderate Negroes understood the general sense of contempt that informed black Americans possessed about what they perceived to be a gross miscarriage of justice. R.R. Moton,

Booker T. Washington's successor, told Washington's former aide Emmett Scott, a Houstonian, that the "general talk among the ordinary Negro is that the Government lynched those soldiers. The feeling is very strong and I have gotten it from a great many different sections and angles. Suppressed emotion is, in some ways, more dangerous than otherwise."[58]

The remaining two courts-martial finished what the first trial started. Fifty-four additional members of the Twenty-fourth stood trial. Of these, only two were acquitted. Twelve men were sentenced to life in prison, twenty four received shorter terms, and sixteen were sentenced to death. This time General Ruckman did not authorize the execution of the men in secret, under cover of darkness. In order to comply with the newly issued General Order Number Seven, which promulgated a new set of rules and procedures concerning the death penalty— enacted as a result of strong black protests and advocacy about the haste and secrecy with which the first thirteen soldiers had been executed—Ruckman postponed punishment until Secretary of War Baker and President Wilson had had an opportunity to review the case. As a result of the review, ten of 16 death sentences were commuted. The remaining six soldiers were hanged in September, 1918 in the same manner in which the first execution was conducted.[59]

Black advocacy, particularly by the NAACP and the black press, to free the remaining convicted soldiers persisted for years. As early as 1918, a "Committee on Public Information," which consisted of thirty-one members of leading black news organizations representing a circulation of more than one million copies, passed a resolution, a "Bill of particulars on which, it is suggested, action might be taken," that demanded executive clemency for the soldiers serving various prison terms at the federal penitentiary in Fort Leavenworth, Kansas.[60] The persistent effort finally paid off: Stewart W. Philips, the last prisoner, was quietly released from the federal prison at Forth Leavenworth in the spring of 1938.[61]

Both Colonel Cress and General Chamberlain, two of the army's investigators of the incident, recommended that Major Snow and a subordinate officer, Captain Lindsey Silvester also be court-martialed.   In an unusually harsh rebuke, General Chamberlain stated that Snow had "exhibited inefficiency and criminal negligence of a character, which...demonstrates his unfitness to command."   General Ruckman chose to ignore the recommendation. Neither officer was convicted, and both were released.

The official investigations and trials following the 1917 Houston Race Riot accomplished the goal of assigning blame for the causes of the violence.   Key individuals were held responsible, executions were carried out, and the white citizenry of Houston was placated. U.S. Army officials, mindful of dozens of previous racial incidents in Brownsville, Rio Grande City, Waco and other locations, worked to mollify public concerns of racial unrest and exerted considerable time and resources to put the wartime incident to rest as quickly and efficiently as possible.

Blacks saw the incident differently and understood that the riot primarily sprung forth not from the pathologies or lack of discipline of disaffected individuals, but from the stifling and enshackling clutches of a Jim Crow system designed to reduce Houston's black population to a state of complete racial subordination.[62]

Blacks understood the real reasons behind the riot and its meaning. They understood the role of racial violence in the Jim Crow system and knew that the Houston riot was not an exception but part of a larger context of state sanctioned racial apartheid.   Thus African Americans were not surprised by subsequent outbreaks of racial violence. For instance when the Harlem Race Riot broke out in 1935, blacks were not surprised by the supposed cause: a rumor, later proven to be false, that the police had beaten to death a teenager accused of stealing a pen knife from a local department store.

Mayor LaGuardia appointed the chair of Howard University's sociology department E. Franklin Frazier to head up an interracial commission to study the causes of the riot. Unlike previous investigations of the sort, the report went well beyond customarily pious denunciations of violence: "This relatively unimportant case of of juvenile pilfering was only the spark that set aflame the smoldering resentments of the people of Harlem against racial discrimination and poverty in the midst of plenty."[63] "The report went on to document the massive exclusion of blacks by all of the city's major employers: the Consolidated Gas Company, the Rapid Transit Company, the hotel industry, the Metropolitan Life Insurance Company, and the unions in the constructions trades, clothing and textiles, and teamsters and chauffeurs."[64]

The first recommendation of the report was that the city "enact an ordinance to the effect that no contracts may be given to any firm or labor union that discriminates against Negro workers."[65] Mayor LaGuardia's response was to suppress the report and to prevent its release to the general public. Black residents of Harlem were disappointed, but not surprised. The report was eventually leaked to the *Amsterdam News*, New York's premier black newspaper, which published it in its entirety.

For his part, Newton Baker's racial views were not affected by the 1917 incident in Houston. In 1935, while serving on the board of the Carnegie Corporation, Baker was the motive force behind the engagement of a Swedish scholar named Gunnar Myrdal to conduct the most lavishly funded and comprehensive investigation of race in American history.[66] In 1936, during contract negotiations with Myrdal, Baker privately wrote Frederick Keppel, the president of the Carnegie Corporation, about the upcoming study. In his letter Baker revealed his true racial attitudes and clearly enunciated his personal beliefs about the institution of slavery. He indicated that he possessed a strong

....feeling of unlimited amazement at the courage of the white people in this country who received the slaves from slave ships and undertook to make useful laborers of them. How many white civilizations could have dared to receive so many wild savages, who were practically uncaged animals, and spread them around over their farms in contact with their own families passes human comprehension. What has been done for the Negro in a hundred years is an unparalleled achievement and nothing but a theoretical democratic impatience can make us critical of it, though, of course, much more remains to be done.[67]

Myrdal's exhaustively researched 1500 page study, *An American Dilemma: The Negro Problem and Modern Democracy*, was published in 1944, sold over 100,000 copies, and went through 25 printings before a second edition was prepared in 1965. Perhaps the strongest pro-integrationist scholarly work in American history, it remains a classic investigation of American race relations, although the funders ensured that Myrdal's study contained no policy recommendations.[68]

History, Responsibility, and Lessons Learned

"For black Texans, questions of myth and history command especially great importance. Like all Afro-Americans they face the dilemma of trying to enter a society that makes too much profit from racism to let them go. Texas myths provide an additional layer of oppression through an idealized portrait of the past which inverts the real historical experience of blacks in the state. In these myths, slaveholders appear as freedom fighters, the pathology of white racism masquerades as individualism, and the cowardly sadism of conquest appears as valor. At the same time, the historical accomplishments of Afro-Americans disappear and the black struggle for citizenship and opportunity becomes transformed into folklore that presents black people as either fools or villains."

—George Lipsitz[1]

Although it came too late for most, the members of the 25th Infantry achieved some measure of redemption for the miscarriage of justice that took place in the aftermath of what happened in Brownsville in 1906. The same cannot be said for the soldiers of the 24th Infantry, and it might be worthwhile to more closely examine why the incident in Houston has historically been seen as more challenging.

Historical causality and assignment of responsibility are always thorny matters; black and white interpretations of the Houston Riot have usually differed in this regard. In this particular case, however, it seems clear that the War Department and the white officers of the Twenty-fourth Infantry bear much of the responsibility for what happened in Houston. The Secretary of War, Newton D. Baker, insisted that the black troops be stationed in the South, over the objections of army officials and officers at multiple levels of the chain of command, and business and civic leaders in the southern cities in which the black troops were to be stationed.[2] The War Department exacerbated the situation by not fully and properly staffing and outfitting the Twenty-fourth regiment—longstanding complaints of the Buffalo soldier regiments since their inception—and by reassigning twenty-five of the regiment's most experienced noncommissioned officers to the commissioned officers school at Fort Des Moines, Iowa. By sending the NCO's away the army may have been responding to activist calls for an increase in the number of black commissioned officers in the regular army, but in doing so alongside its insistence to station the black troops in a hostile environment it all but assured the unfolding of violent confrontation. For their part, the NCO's being trained at Fort Des Moines were distraught when they learned that their regiment had mutinied and rioted and believed that if they had been with their men the Houston incident would not have occurred. They even volunteered to "give up their prospects for commissions so as to return to the regiment and redeem its reputation."[3]

The War Department also bears responsibility for transferring command of the Twenty-fourth from Col. William Newman, a mediocre but competent officer with experience commanding black troops, to Maj. Kneeland Snow, an inept, dishonest, and thoughtless man who testified against his own troops during the trial and who was usually away from camp enjoying Houston's nightlife instead of looking after his troops.

The Houston business establishment must also accept some of the blame for what happened. In hindsight, the assurances of boosters at the chamber of commerce that the soldiers would be treated well by Houston's white community seem disingenuous. Ben Davidson and other leading Houstonians knew full well that their police force was comprised of racist thugs who enjoyed terrorizing the local black community, yet they not only did nothing but passively and actively encourage the practice. Even after it became clear that tensions between the soldiers, white construction workers, and the police were reaching the boiling point, the city's business leaders kept silent, afraid of risking the much desired influx of federal dollars the construction of Camp Logan and the airfield represented.

It has been suggested that the rioting soldiers of the Twenty-fourth must shoulder at least some share of the responsibility. Robert V. Haynes, author of *A Night of Violence: The Houston Riot of 1917* and other authors, usually white, argue that the men, as soldiers, had the duty to submit to Houston's Jim Crow laws and customs and did not have the right to take the law into their own hands. It has also been pointed out that the army's controversial and secret execution of the men after the first trial was legal and fully in keeping with army rules and regulations of the time.[4] Adherents of these views, however, usually omit some important facts and must contend with some compelling counter-arguments:

1. The army of the time was a racist institution and its rules, regulations, and military traditions reflected longstanding customs and practices of both written and unwritten prejudice against black soldiers. Pointing out that the army followed its own rules, therefore, is similar to saying that the segregationist practices endemic to American society in the 1950's and 1960's too were "legal." Legal sufficiency is not the sole standard with which to judge human and civil rights matters, especially during the Jim Crow era.

2. White mutineers and deserters, which have been a part of the U.S. military since its inception, often received lighter sentences than black soldiers for the same or similar offenses, particularly in frontier or overseas locations, a fact not lost on black soldiers. This does not excuse the act of mutiny, but it does suggest that the soldiers of the Twenty-fourth would have been treated rather differently, at every stage of their time in Houston, had they been white.

FIGURE 6.1. Headstone of Corporal Charles Baltimore at Fort Sam Houston National Cemetery, San Antonio, Texas. Note that the marker omits Baltimore's birthdate as well as his rank. The other soldiers that were executed lie nearby. Photo by the author.

3. In spite of multiple investigations, three trials, and nineteen executions, none of the accused were ever actually positively identified by anyone as participants in the riot. The basis for the convictions was questionable testimony from junior enlisted soldiers who had only been wearing a soldier's uniform for a few months and who could be coerced into testifying against their fellow soldiers, a tactic that was also tried in the Brownsville incident but failed. In both cases efforts on the part of prosecutors to secure convictions relied on a race based double-standard: the presumption of collective as opposed to individual guilt.

4. Racist victimization produces physiological and psychological consequences. The cumulative impact of Jim Crow in Houston and the total failure of institutions and support systems that could have furnished the soldiers with some

recourse, left the soldiers feeling deserted and under attack. The heavy weight of racism both within and outside the army was a form of traumatic stress that the junior enlisted men of the Twenty-fourth simply were not emotionally equipped to deal with.[5]

5. At the time of the "nadir" of race relations, the army did not see itself as an agent of positive social change on the race question. This is particularly unfortunate because given the economic importance of Camp Logan and Ellington Field to the city of Houston, the army could have forced local officials to treat the soldiers of the Twenty-fourth with dignity and respect. When Emmett J. Scott, who also served as Newton Baker's special assistant for minority affairs after his mentor Booker T. Washington died, asked the War Department to implement more humane racial policies in the wake of the incident at Houston, Baker replied "There is no intention on the part of the War Department to undertake at this time a settlement of the so-called race question."[6]

Even after the issuance of Executive Order 9981 following World War II, which integrated the military and mandated equality of treatment and opportunity (it also made it illegal, per military law, to make a racist remark), Twenty-fourth Infantry soldiers such as Leon Gilbert found themselves facing a court-martial during the Korean War, for reasons similar to the charges faced by the Houston mutineers.[7] As the army would find out during the Vietnam War, and the Navy would later learn during its efforts to reform fleet personnel policies in the 1970's following a series of racial uprisings onboard ships, the real problem was institutional racism within the service, not isolated incidents of racial tension that would occasionally explode like a volcano.[8]

Associated Historic Sites

Readers interested in visiting sites associated with the Houston Riot can choose from a variety of locations. Among the most prominent are the following:

FIGURE 6.2 Camp Logan Historical Marker. Photo by the author.

1. Memorial Park (former site of Camp Logan)
2. Fort Sam Houston National Cemetery (burial site of most of the executed soldiers), and
3. Freedmen's Town Historic District, Houston. Most of the district has been gentrified, but enough of it remains to form useful first-hand impressions.

Notes

Introduction

[1] Rayford Logan, The Betrayal of the Negro (New York: MacMillan, 1970); Eric Foner, Reconstruction: America's Unfinished Revolution (New York: Perennial, 1988), 604.

[2] Geoffrey C. Ward, Unforgivable Blackness: The Rise and Fall of Jack Johnson (New York: Vintage), 215-216. Theresa Rundstedtler, Jack Johnson, Rebel Sojourner (Berkeley, University of California Press, 2012).

Chapter One

[1] Garna L. Christian, Black Soldiers in Jim Crow Texas, 1899-1917 (College Station: Texas A&M University Press, 1995), xiii.

[2] Bruce Glasrud, Western Black Soldiers since the Buffalo Soldiers: A Review of the Literature, in Buffalo Soldiers in the West, Bruce Glasrud and Michael N. Searles, eds., (College Station: Texas A&M University Press, 2007), 6-30; Christian, xiii.

[3] Garna L. Christian, Black Soldiers in Jim Crow Texas, 1899-1917 (College Station: Texas A&M University Press, 1995), xiii.

[4] Robert V. Haynes, A Night of Violence: The Houston Riot of 1917 (Baton Rouge: Louisiana State University Press, 1976), 9.

[5] John Hope Franklin and Alfred A Moss, Jr., From Slavery to Freedom: A History of African Americans (7th ed.), 300.

[6] Willard B. Gatewood, Jr. "Negro Troops in Florida, 1898," Florida Historical Quarterly, XLIX (July 1970), 1-15; Haynes, 11.

[7] Christian, 116-117.

[8] It may be helpful to bear in mind that both the battles of El Caney and San Juan Hill involved numerically superior American forces. In the former battle, 600 Spanish soldiers defended their position against over 6,000 Americans and inflicted over 400 casualties. At San Juan Hill confusion and delay resulted in severe U.S. casualties until Colonel Roosevelt and his men, supported by

the Tenth Cavalry, successfully charged Kettle Hill and San Juan Heights, securing the American position. Altogether there were 5,462 American deaths in the war, only 379 of which were battle casualties. The rest died from yellow fever, malaria, dysentery and other diseases. Tainted meat sold to the government by the Armour Company may have also killed some American troops. Kenneth C. Davis, Don't Know Much About History: Everything you need to know about American history but never learned (New York: Perennial, 2004), 288-289; Willard B. Gatewood, Jr., Black Americans and the White Man's Burden, 1898-1903, (Urbana: University of Illinois Press, 1975, 106-107.

[9] James R. Leiker, Racial Borders: Black Soldiers along the Rio Grande, College Station: Texas A&M University Press, 2002, 28-29, 82-83, 109; Willard B. Gatewood, Jr., "Black Americans and the Quest for Empire, 1898-1903." Journal of Southern History 38 (1972), 545-66; Gerald Horne, Black and Brown: African Americans and the Mexican Revolution, 1910-1920, 92.

[10] During the earlier portions of the Spanish-American War, the ties between the black troops and the Afro-Cuban and Puerto Rican civilian population were significant. That "splendid little war" was portrayed as a war of liberation, and Buffalo Soldiers took great pride in liberating another people of color, even if white political leaders and soldiers bemoaned the fact that so many of the Cuban freedom fighters were Negroes. The Philippine Insurrection, on the other hand, was a guerilla conflict that lasted for years and had all of the hallmarks of an imperial war: an aroused indigenous population, massive military and civilian casualties, war atrocities, and race-based brutality, all of which helped to create the environment under which some of the soldiers of the Twenty-fourth such as David Fagan defected and joined Emiliano Aguinaldo and his Filipino forces. Haynes, 13; Manila Times, June 29, 1902; Gatewood, Jr. (1975), 154-156.

[11] Haynes, 15; William G. Muller, The Twenty-Fourth Infantry: Past and Present, 78-81.

Chapter Two

[1] Joseph Benson Foraker, Notes of a Busy Life (Cincinnati: Stewart & Kidd Company, 1916), 231-232; John D. Weaver, The Brownsville Raid (New York: W. W. Norton & Co., Inc., 1973), 15, 96; Message from the President of the United States, Part 1 (60th U.S. Congress, Senate Document No. 402, 1908), 183; Message from the President of the United States, Part 2 (60th U.S. Congress, Senate Document No. 402, 1908), ii; Message from the President of the United States (59th U.S. Congress, Senate Document No. 155, 1908), 3.
[2] Weaver, 116, 145, 166.
[3] Joseph Benson Foraker, A Review of Testimony in the Brownsville Investigation (The North American Review, Vol. 187, No. 629, pp. 550-558, 1908), 550-551.
[4] Weaver, 321-322.

Chapter Three

[1] Robert Wooster, "TWENTY-FIFTH UNITED STATES INFANTRY," Handbook of Texas Online (http://www.tshaonline.org/handbook/online/articles/qlt02), accessed April 03, 2011. Published by the Texas State Historical Association.
[2] Weaver, 18.
[3] Weaver, 19-20; Alicia A. Garza and Christopher Long, "BROWNSVILLE, TX," Handbook of Texas Online (http://www.tshaonline.org/handbook/online/articles/hdb04), accessed April 06, 2011. Published by the Texas State Historical Association.
[4] Wikipedia, "Brownsville, Texas" (http://en.wikipedia.org/wiki/Brownsville,_Texas), accessed July 11, 2011; Anders Stephanson, Manifest Destiny: American Expansion and the Empire of Right. (New York: Hill and Wang, 1996), 35-40.
[5] Garna L. Christian, Black Soldiers in Jim Crow Texas, 1899-1917 (College Station: Texas A&M University Press, 1995), 71.

[6] Weaver, 20; Gerald Horne, Black and Brown: African Americans and the Mexican Revolution, 1910-1920 (New York: NYU Press, 2005), 16.

[7] Anne Cowling, The Civil War Trade of the Lower Rio Grande Valley. (Unpublished Masters Thesis, University of Texas at Austin, 1926).

[8] "Mexican women, particularly those of easy virtue, often befriended the black soldiers, sending Latin tempers soaring. The towns of South Texas at century's end drew like a magnet societal dregs from both sides of the border who engaged in an assortment of nefarious activities. To them the military presented an obstacle to their profitable pursuits." Garna L. Christian, "Rio Grande City: Prelude to the Brownsville Raid." Buffalo Soldiers in the West: A Black Soldiers Anthology edited by Bruce A. Glasrud and Michael N. Searles. (College Station, TX: Texas A&M University Press, 2007), 186-187.

[9] Garna L. Christian, Black Soldiers in Jim Crow Texas, 1899-1917 (College Station: Texas A&M University Press, 1995), 72; Frank N. Schubert, Voices of the Buffalo Soldier: Records, Reports and Recollections of Military Life and Service in the West. (Albuquerque: University of New Mexico Press, 2003), 244-246.

[10] Weaver, 270; John Hope Franklin and Alfred A Moss, Jr., From Slavery to Freedom: A History of African Americans (7th ed.), 312.

[11] Anita Tillman, "A Step Back for Blacks." Time, July 3, 2006. Online at http://www.time.com/time/magazine/article/0,9171,1207828,00.html, accessed April 8, 2011.

[12] Christian, 2007, 186-188.

[13] The soldiers were to have stopped off in Austin for training with the Texas National Guard on their way to Fort Brown, but the regiment's white officers and black chaplain protested due to the problematic racial climate in Texas, leading the War Department to revoke the temporary stopover in Austin. Jack D. Foner, Blacks and the Military in American History, (New York: Praeger Publishers, 1974), 96.

[14] Weaver, 18-22, 25, 28, 172.

[15] Foraker (1916), 232.

[16] Weaver, 29-30.

[17] Weaver, 31; Christian, 2007, 73.

[18] Gerald Astor, The Right to Fight: A History of African Americans in the Military. (New York, Da Capo Press, 2001), 81.

[19] Astor, 87

[20] Foraker (1916), 232; Weaver, 35-36.

[21] Weaver, 61-62, 71.

[22] Christian, 1995, 73.

[23] Weaver, 47, 50, 65.

[24] Foraker (1916), 232; Weaver, 62, 63, 66, 72.

[25] Foraker (1916), 232; Weaver, 74-76.

[26] Weaver, 76, 89.

[27] Foraker (1916), 265; Message from the President of the United States, Part 2 (60th U.S. Congress, Senate Document No. 402, 1908), vii-xviii.

[28] Tillman, 2006.

[29] Cited in Christian, 1995, 74.

[30] Austin Statesman, August 16, 1906.

[31] Vance H. Marchbanks, "A Soldier's Opinion of the Recent Excitement at Brownsville, Tex." The Voice of the Negro 3 (December 1906), 549.

[32] Weaver, 80.

[33] Weaver, 85-86. Originally from Mississippi and the son of a Confederate soldier who died at the Battle of Corinth, McDonald relocated to Texas after the Civil War. McDonald worked as a bodyguard for both Presidents Theodore Roosevelt and Woodrow Wilson, with Roosevelt writing the introduction to McDonald's 1909 biography. Harold J. Weiss, Yours to Command: The Life and Legend of Texas Ranger Captain Bill McDonald (Denton, TX: University of North Texas Press, 2009); Albert Bigelow Paine, Captain Bill McDonald, a Texas Ranger: A Story of Frontier Reform (New York: J. J. Little & Ives Co., 1909).

[34] Weaver, 91.

[35] Foraker (1916), 233.

[36] Message from the President of the United States, Part 1 (60th U.S. Congress, Senate Document No. 402, 1908), 182.

[37] Thornbrough, Emma Lou, The Brownsville Episode and the Negro Vote (The Mississippi Valley Historical Review, Vol. 44, No. 3, pp. 469-493, 1957), 470; Tinsley, James A., Roosevelt, Foraker, and

the Brownsville Affray (The Journal of Negro History, Vol. 41, No. 1, pp. 43-65), p. 47.

[38] Message from the President of the United States, Part 1 (60th U.S. Congress, Senate Document No. 402, 1908), 183.

[39] New York Age, November 8, 1906.

[40] Franklin and Moss, 315.

[41] In the spring of 1912, when President Taft was in political trouble back home, he found Mingo Sanders working for the federal government as a day laborer at a dollar seventy-five cents a day. Weaver 121, 242-245.

[42] Foraker (1916), 246.

[43] Thornbrough, 470-474.

[44] When Roosevelt insisted that he would have treated white troops exactly the same way, Booker T. Washington, the so-called "Wizard of Tuskegee" decided to continue his dependable support of the president and the Republican party, to the consternation of not just black activists such as Du Bois and McGhee, but the Afro-American rank and file as well. Weaver, 273-275.

[45] Weaver, 274; David Levering Lewis, W.E.B. Du Bois: Biography of a Race. (New York: Henry Holt, 1993), 330-333.

[46] Weaver, 273; Oberlin Tribune, September 4, 1908.

[47] Thornbrough, 470; Weaver, 99, 274.

[48] Cited in Foner, 99.

[49] Foner, 99-100.

[50] Weaver, 113.

[51] A recent study of the Brownsville Affair argues that Captain Macklin should have been found guilty at trial and that he could have been the person who fired the pistol shots that started the riot. Ricardo Purnell Malbrew, Brownsville Revisited, unpublished Master's Thesis, Louisiana State University, 2007. Even Texas Ranger McDonald thought that Macklin potentially plaid a role in the riot. Anne J. Lane, The Brownsville Affair (New York: Kennikat Press, 1971), 19.

[52] Foraker (1908), 555-558; Foraker (1916) 277-291.

[53] Weaver, 183.

[54] Weaver, 182-184.

[55] Weaver 192-206.

[56] Weaver, 213-233.
[57] Weaver, 224-225.
[58] Weaver, 224-225, 248.
[59] Foner, 102.
[60] Tinsley; Thornbrough

Chapter Four

[1] C. Calvin Smith, The Houston Riot of 1917, Revisited, in Buffalo Soldiers in the West, Bruce Glasrud and Michael N. Searles, eds., (College Station: Texas A&M University Press, 2007), 199.
[2] W. D. Carrigan, W. D. The Making of a Lynching Culture: Violence and Vigilantism in Central Texas 1836-1916. (Urbana and Chicago: University of Illinois Press, 2004).
[3] Robert Perkinson, Texas Tough: The Rise of America's Prison Empire. (New York: Metropolitan Books, 2010).
[4] John Minton (n.d.). The Houston Riot and Courts-Martial of 1917. San Antonio: Institute of Texan Cultures, 3.
[5] Lt. Col. (Ret.) Michael Lee Lanning, The African-American Soldier: From Crispus Attucks to Colin Powell. New York: Citadel Press, 1997), 126.

Chapter Five

[1] Houston City Directory, 1918, 7-8; Marilyn McAdams Sibley, Port of Houston: A History (Austin and London: 1968), 146-48.
[2] David G. McComb, "HOUSTON, TX," Handbook of Texas Online (http://www.tshaonline.org/handbook/online/articles/hdh03), accessed February 21, 2011; Howard Beeth and Cary D. Wintz (eds.) Black Dixie: Afro-Texan History and Culture in Houston, 89; Haynes 16-17.
[3] Beeth and Wintz, 89.
[4] Martha Gruening, "Houston: An N.A.A.C.P. Investigation," Crisis 15 (November 1917), 17.
[5] Haynes, 84.
[6] Garna L. Christian, Black Soldiers in Jim Crow Texas, 1899-1917 (College Station: Texas A&M University Press, 1995), 146.

[7] Haynes, 18.

[8] Haynes, 21; Houston Post, August 1, 3, 18, 1917.

[9] Advocates of prohibition placed an advertisement in the August 20, 1917 Houston Post that sought to link their campaign efforts with the anticipated arrival of the black troops. Their advertisement read as follows:

3,000 NEGRO TROOPS TO BE IN HOUSTON WITHIN THE MONTH

Can the men of Harris County afford to vote to continue the saloon in the face of this? For the security of the homes of this community and for the protection of the law-abiding negro, who be helpless

MAKE HARRIS COUNTY DRY—
REMEMBER BROWNSVILLE

Harris County, Local Option Committee,
A.S. Moody, Vice Chairman

The explicit reference to the Brownsville Riot of 1906 was a transparent and unfortunate play on racial fear, and revealed much about the race relations climate in Houston prior to the arrival of the troops. Houston Post, August 20, 1917.

[10] Haynes, 30; Houston Press, March 20, 1917; Houston Chronicle, June 15, 1917.

[11] National Archivers and Records Administration. "The Zimmerman Telegram," (http://www.archives.gov/education/lessons/zimmermann/), accessed February 25, 2011.

[12] Haynes, 48; Houston Chronicle, May 16, 20, 1917.

[13] Houston Chronicle, June 11, 1917; Houston Press, June 12, 1917.

[14] Houston Chronicle, August 26, 1917; Christian, 148, Robert V. Haynes, "The Houston Mutiny and Riot of 1917," Southwestern Historical Quarterly 76 (1973), 420.

[15] President Woodrow Wilson was a committed segregationist who considered the Negro question a "human problem" not a political one. When a delegation of blacks led by William Monroe Trotter protested Wilson's discriminatory actions, particularly his

re-segregation of the federal government (the first since 1863), he told them "segregation is not a humiliation but a benefit, and ought to be so regarded by you gentlemen." "President Resents Negro's Criticism." The New York Times, November 13, 1914.

[16] John Hope Franklin and Alfred A Moss, Jr., From Slavery to Freedom: A History of African Americans (7th ed.), (New York: McGraw-Hill, 1994) 323-330; Craig Lloyd, Eugene Bullard: Black Expatriate in Jazz-Age Paris (Athens, GA: University of Georgia Press, 2006).

[17] Hal S. Chase, "Struggle for Equality: Fort Des Moines Training Camp for Colored Officers, 1917," Phylon, Vol. 39, No. 4 (4th Qtr., 1978), pp. 297-310; David Levering Lewis, W.E.B. Du Bois: Biography of a Race, 1868-1919 (New York: Henry Holt, 1993), 542; Robin D.G. Kelley and Earl Lewis (Eds.), To Make Our World Anew: A History of African Americans (New York: Oxford University Press, 2000), 330-331.

[18] Haynes, 36-37.

[19] Haynes, 38, 39; Smith, 210.

[20] Mennell, 284.

[21] James Mennell, "African-Americans and the Selective Service Act of 1917," The Journal of Negro History, Vol. 84, No. 3 (Summer, 1999), pp. 275-287.

[22] Smith, 199.

[23] Haynes, 64. This story, which was never corroborated, appears to have been fabricated after the riot in order to shift blame for the cause of the mutiny from the racist Houston police force onto the soldiers.

[24] Five soldiers were dishonorably discharged and each was given a five-year sentence at hard labor. A sixth soldier was sentenced to ten years in prison. P.S. Ruckman, "John Wilson Ruckman" (http://psruckman.com/JWR.htm), accessed March 30, 2011.

[25] Haynes, 67-68, Christian, 151.

[26] Lieutenant William Chaffin, the battalion medical officer was especially disgusted when he overheard one white Houstonian comment that "in Texas it costs twenty-five dollars to kill a buzzard and five dollars to kill a nigger." Haynes 74.

[27] Haynes 78; Testimony of William Bixley, Cress Report, Appendix B. Houston Press, August 19, 1917.

[28] Haynes, 79-80.

[29] Testimony of General John A. Huhlen, August 24, 1917, Cress Report; Haynes 76.

[30] Haynes, 75-76.

[31] According to Travers when she asked Sparks why they had broken into her home he replied "Don't you ask an officer want he want in your house. I'm from Fort Ben [Fort Bend County, a historical center of plantation slavery in Texas] and we don't allow niggers to talk back to us." Daniels then charged into the home and asked what was to be done with the black woman. Sparks responded "Take and give her ninety days on the Pea Farm 'cause she's one of these biggety nigger women." Sparks was referring to Texas's well established system of plantation based convict leasing, a cornerstone of white supremacy during this time period. Perkinson, 1-10; Douglas A. Blackmon, Slavery by Another Name: The Re-Enslavement of Black Americans from the Civil War to World War II (New York: Doubleday, 2008); Gruening, 15; Christian, 151; Robert V. Haynes, "The Houston Mutiny and Riot of 1917," Southwestern Historical Quarterly 76 (1973), 427; Edgar A. Schuler, The Houston Race Riot, 1917. Journal of Negro History, Vol. XXIX, No. 3, July 1944, 316.

[32] Christian, 151; U.S. v. William C. Nesbit, Sergeant, Company I, 24th Infantry, et al. Fort Sam Houston, Texas, Nov. 1., 1917, Judge Advocate General's Office, U.S. War Department, RG 153, N.A.

[33] Smith 203; Cress Report, October 5, 1917, RG 401. Sparks was shocked when Brock informed him of his overnight suspension. Despite a well-known reputation for racist brutality, he had never been suspended before for his terroristic threatening of Houston's black population, although he had recently served a ten day suspension without pay for "improper remarks made to a white woman." He accused Brock of being a "nigger lover" and angrily declared that "any man who sticks up for a nigger is no better than a nigger." Smith, 204.

[34] Christian, 154.

[35] Haynes, 179.

[36] Colonel John S. Hoover, commanding officer of the Fifth Texas Infantry, found Brock in a complete state of confusion at 11:45 [p.m.] when he tried to confer with him and acting mayor Dan Moody. "We talked with Chief of Police Brock," Hoover recalled, "but couldn't get any information out of him one way or the other. He was absolutely helpless. Hoover was especially shocked when Brock could not even tell him the number of police officers on duty. Haynes, 179.

[37] Christian, 159.

[38] Houston Post, September 12, 1917; Christian, 159.

[39] Houston Post, August 28, 1917; Schuler, 336.

[40] Haynes, 200.

[41] Gruening, 16.

[42] Gruening, 17.

[43] Newman's policy of allowing civilians onto Camp Logan, itself an adjustment to the prevailing Jim Crow conditions of Houston, later opened the army up to charges of fostering drinking and prostitution. The army's own investigation of the incident differed from the civilian inquiry on this point and found that Newman's actions in this regard had been reasonable given the circumstances. "The charges that Newman's policies had turned the camp into a veritable red light district were made after the mutiny and riot and not before it." Haynes, 45.

[44] Haynes, 208.

[45] Christian, 162.

[46] John Minton (n.d.). The Houston Riot and Courts-Martial of 1917. San Antonio: Institute of Texan Cultures; Smith, 207; Christian 163.

[47] Haynes, 266.

[48] Haynes, 249-50.

[49] P.S. Ruckman, "John Wilson Ruckman" (http://psruckman.com/JWR.htm), accessed March 30, 2011.

[50] The court consisted of three brigadier generals, seven colonels, and three lieutenant colonels. Of these five were northerners, four were southerners, and four were westerners. Eight of the thirteen were graduates of West Point. Marguerite Johnson, Houston: The Unknown City, 1836-1946 (College Station: Texas A&M University Press), 203.

[51] Haynes, 258; Houston Chronicle, November 2, 3, 4, 6, 1917; testimony of Major Kneeland Snow, U.S. v. Nesbit, 44, 47-48, 60-68.

[52] For photographs of their headstones, taken February 9, 2011, see Appendix A.

[53] Minton, 16; Haynes, 273.

[54] W.E.B. Du Bois, The Crisis, 14 (Number 6, October 1917), 284-285; Horne, 75.

[55] Baltimore Afro-American, September 1, 1917, 1.

[56] Cited in John Hope Franklin and Alfred A. Moss, Jr. From Slavery to Freedom: A History of African Americans (7th ed.). (New York: McGraw Hill), 330.

[57] W.E.B. Du Bois, The Crisis, 15 (Number 3, January, 1918), 114; W.C. Lloyd, The Crisis, 15 (Number 3, January 1918), 130-31.

[58] Horne, 75; R.R. Moton to Emmett Scott, undated, Record Group 107, Box 1, File M, Emmett Scott Papers, National Archives and Records Administration, College Park, Maryland.

[59] Minton, 26; Haynes, 278-79.

[60] Address to the Committee on Public Information, in Herbert Aptheker, A Documentary History of the Negro People in the United States, Vol. 3. (Secaucus, NJ: Citadel Press), 218-222.

[61] Chicago Defender, April 30, 1938.

[62] Not every black person felt this way. At the time of the incident Henry O. Flipper, West Point's first black graduate, was living in El Paso Texas and was asked his opinion about the riot. He was quoted in the Negro press as saying that "the men of the Twenty-fourth Infantry are gamblers, thugs, bums and the scum of our people." In response the editor of The Crisis felt it necessary to opine that "it is...unfortunate that reputable colored American papers should publish such a libel. There is an abundance of testimony that the men of the Twenty-fourth Regiment are in the main brave and honest men and just as worthy of the respect of their race and nation as Henry O. Flipper." W.E.B. Du Bois, Crisis 15 (November 1917), 12.

[63] E. Franklin Frazier, The Negro in Harlem: A Report on Social and Economic Conditions Responsible for the Outbreak of March 19, 1935. (New York: Arno Press, 1968), 7; John Hope Franklin and Alfred A. Moss, Jr. From Slavery to Freedom: A

History of African Americans (7th ed.). (New York: McGraw Hill, 1994), 400.

[64] Stephen Steinberg, Race Relations, A Critique. (Stanford, CA: Stanford University Press, 2007), 68.

[65] Frazier, 129.

[66] The Carnegie Corporation was one of many organizations created by businessman and philanthropist Andrew Carnegie, one of Booker T. Washington's most significant patrons. Leslie G. Carr, Color-Blind Racism (Thousand Oaks, CA: Sage Publications), 72-73.

[67] Quoted in Walter Jackson, Gunnar Myrdal and America's Conscience: Social Engineering & Racial Liberalism, 1938-1987. (Chapel Hill: University of North Carolina Press, 1990), 21; Steinberg, 84-85. Further insight into Baker's character can be obtained by examining some of his public pronouncements concerning young people during the Great Depression. Beginning in 1931 both high school and college enrollments throughout the United States began dropping dramatically, as young people had to find work to support often starving families. At a time of profound crisis for America's young people —the president's advisory commission on education warned of a whole "lost generation of young people"—Baker maintained that there was "plenty of opportunity for young people of initiative and spirit to earn a living." Baker's rather idiosyncratic claim drew a sarcastic response from First Lady Eleanor Roosevelt who sarcastically wrote to Baker "I confess that my own imagination has been extremely lacking for the last few months! If you have any convincing suggestions....I shall be more than grateful." Baker had no such suggestions. Robert A. Caro, The Path to Power, (New York: Vintage), 343.

[68] Du Bois publicly praised Myrdal's "monumental study, which he knew broke important ground. Privately, however, he understood that Myrdal's study had significant shortcomings. David Levering Lewis, W.E.B. Du Bois: The Fight for Equality and the American Century, 1919-1963, (New York: Henry Holt, 2000), 448-453.

Conclusion

[1] Goin' On: Afro-American Imagery in Texas Film and Folklore," Southwest Media Review 3 (Spring, 1985). Cited in Beeth & Wintz Black Dixie: Afro-Texan History and Culture in Houston, pp. 7-8

[2] Baker, a lawyer and former mayor of Cleveland, was a strong supporter of President Wilson, having met him while both were at Johns Hopkins in the 1890's. The son of a Confederate soldier, Baker also shared Wilson's retrograde racial attitudes. While his political and administrative skills were held in high regard, he freely admitted to knowing next to nothing about the military, and was not held in high regard by most men in uniform. It is entirely possible he saw his decision to station black troops in the south almost purely in administrative rather than military terms. Wikipedia, "Newton D. Baker" (http://en.wikipedia.org/wiki/Newton_Baker), accessed March 31, 2011; Newton Diehl Baker Papers, National Archives.

[3] Brig. General J. L. Chamberlain, Inspector General, U.S. Army to Adjutant General, September 26, 1917, Record Group 407, Records of the Adjutant General's Office, Box 1277, National Archives; Smith, 210.

[4] Although the army, according to Henry Sands who has written a screenplay about the riot, refused to grant full access to the trial transcripts and investigation reports for fifty years following the trial. Henry Sands, Houston Adjustment: A screenplay about the Houston Riots of 1917. (http://www.amazon.com/Houston-Adjustment-screenplay-about-ebook/dp/B004LDL93O), accessed March 31, 2011.

[5] International Society for Traumatic Stress Studies, "What is Traumatic Stress?" (http://www.istss.org/WhatisTrauma/2753.htm), accessed March 30, 2011.

[6] Smith, 210-211; David M. Kennedy, Over Here: The First World War and American Society. (New York Oxford University Press, 1980), 159.

[7] Another noteworthy Jim Crow court-martial involving a black soldier was the trial of Second Lieutenant Jackie Roosevelt

Robinson, who, accompanied by the light-skinned wife of a fellow officer, refused a white bus conductor's order to sit in the back of a segregated bus while stationed at Fort Hood, Texas on July 6, 1944.   Jules Tygiel, The Court-Martial of Jackie Robinson. American Heritage Magazine, August/September 1984, Volume 35, Issue 5; Wikipedia, "Leon Gilbert." (http://en.wikipedia.org/wiki/Leon_Gilbert), accessed March 31, 2011.

[8] Elmo Zumwalt, Jr., On Watch. (New York: Quadrangle, 1976); John Darrell Sherwood, Black Sailor, White Navy: Racial Unrest in the Fleet During the Vietnam War Era.   (New York: New York University Press, 2007).

Made in the USA
Columbia, SC
13 January 2022

53511319R00052